INVADING THE DARKNESS

Inside the Historic Fight Against Child Sex Trafficking
in the United States

by

Linda Smith

Some names have been changed to protect the identities of the men, women and children we serve.

ISBN 978-0-9896451-5-7

Cover and text design by Sean Allen; Text layouts by J David Ford and Associates.

© 2018 Shared Hope International

Printed in the United States of America.

Shared Hope International
P.O. Box 65337
Vancouver, WA 98665
www.sharedhope.org

ACKNOWLEDGEMENTS

There are many more people I would like to thank than can be included in one book. Some have received little or no credit for their hard work in this movement while others are powerful figures who've used their voices to shine the spotlight of awareness to a public unaware. Some have worked tirelessly over the past decades, and some contributed for a time their sweat and tears. I wish there could be an acknowledgement to every one of them, because every person has been needed, every voice important, and every contribution essential.

But for the completion of this particular project, I must acknowledge these individuals: the varied and incredible contributors that you'll discover in these chapters from Ernie Allen, Drew Oosterbaan, Deborah Richardson, Amy O'Neill Richard, Samantha Healy Vardaman, Melissa Snow, Kristy Childs, and Nancy Winston; the writer, Cindy Coloma, who has traveled this long journey and many versions with me; and the diligent staff and former staff and interns at Shared Hope International — in particular, Marissa Gunther, MSW and the *Invading the Darkness* Project Manager, and Christine Raino, Esq., Senior Director of Public Policy and the SHI Center for Justice and Advocacy, who has been an invaluable and unsung resource throughout this process of checking laws and accuracy. My deepest appreciation to each one of you.

TABLE OF CONTENTS

Chapter 1 – Cries from the Shadows — *Linda Smith, U.S. Congress 1995-99, Washington State Senate/House 1983-94, Founder and President of Shared Hope International* *1*

Chapter 2 – The Knock on his Office Door — *Ernie Allen, Founding Chairman and Former President, National Center for Missing & Exploited Children; working with administrations from President Ronald Reagan to President Barack Obama* *13*

Chapter 3 – A Victim's Story *19*

Chapter 4 – Missing Kids in America — *Ernie Allen, Founding Chairman and Former President, National Center for Missing & Exploited Children; working with administrations from President Ronald Reagan to President Barack Obama* *23*

Chapter 5 – The Modern U.S. Abolitionists — *Amy O'Neill Richard, Senior Advisor to the Director, Office to Monitor and Combat Trafficking in Persons (J/TIP), serving under Presidents Bill Clinton, George W. Bush, Barack Obama, and Donald Trump* *41*

Chapter 6 – Atlanta's Child in Shackles — *Deborah Richardson, Founder and Executive Director of International Human Trafficking Institute* *59*

Chapter 7 – A Victim's Story *69*

Chapter 8 – Trafficking Dynamics — *Samantha Healy Vardaman, General Counsel, Shared Hope International* *75*

Chapter 9 – A Victim's Story *85*

Chapter 10 – Seeking Justice — *Drew Oosterbaan, Former Chief of Child Exploitation and Obscenity Section of the U.S. Department of Justice, 2001–2015 serving under Presidents Bill Clinton, George W. Bush, and Barack Obama* *93*

Chapter 11 – Justice at Work — *Drew Oosterbaan, Former Chief of Child Exploitation and Obscenity Section of the U.S. Department of Justice, 2001–2015 serving under Presidents Bill Clinton, George W. Bush, and Barack Obama* *109*

Chapter 12 – Identifying Victims to Change Lives — *Melissa Snow, Director of Programs at Shared Hope International; Child Sex Trafficking Program Specialist, National Center for Missing and Exploited Children; Federal Child Victim Assistance Program Coordinator* *135*

Chapter 13 – Who Buys a Child for Sex? *151*

Chapter 14 – The Battle for Our Children's Minds *159*

Chapter 15 – Brianna's Close Call *167*

Chapter 16 – Victims Charged with the Crime that Victimized Them ... *181*

Chapter 17 – A Survivor's Story *187*

Chapter 18 – Changing Culture, Changing Lives *195*

Chapter 19 – Online Predators and The Porn Connection *205*

Chapter 20 – The Forgotten Victims, Boys & Men — *Judge Robert Lung, member of U.S. Presidential Advisory Council on Human Trafficking* *215*

Chapter 21 – The Sex-Trafficking Movement From a Survivor's Perspective — *Kristy Childs, Founder and President of Veronica's Voice, Inc.* *231*

Chapter 22 – The Essential Voices, Survivors — *Nancy Winston, LGSW, Vice President of Shared Hope International, Emeritus Board* *247*

Chapter 23 – A Look at the Wins *259*

Chapter 24 – Lights in the Darkness *267*

NOTE TO READERS

The fight against child sex trafficking in America has endured for well over a century. Though the issue has been known by various names and descriptions throughout its history, every era has had its notable sea-changers. The people and organizations this book highlights did not begin the fight but have had a significant impact in bringing about the advances in justice we have seen in the past two decades.

This book is drawn from numerous authoritative sources including interviews, published materials, government archives, research, police records, and first-person recollections. Scenes that are stated as being victim or survivor stories have been recreated from these sources. Some names and locations have been changed.

"THE HISTORY OF THIS ISSUE IS A HISTORY OF INDIVIDUALS."

DREW OOSTERBAAN

Chief of Child Exploitation and Obscenity Section of the U.S. Department of Justice (2001–2015)

1

CRIES FROM THE SHADOWS

Linda Smith, U.S. Congress 1995-99, Washington State Senate/House 1983-94, Founder and President of Shared Hope International

"FOR GOD'S SAKE DO SOMETHING!"
1910 QUOTE BY GENERAL BOOTH, FOUNDER OF THE SALVATION ARMY

American kids are being sold for sex.

This isn't a new problem in our country. Back in the early 1900s, General Booth of the Salvation Army gave this call to action to "do something!"

During this time, a movement had risen up across the United States of America in response to hearing about girls and women being forced or coerced into prostitution — what we now call sex trafficking. These were often young women of humble means given promises of good jobs in the cities. They were immigrants arriving from Europe seeking a better life in America and met at the docks by respectable-looking people promising to help. They were young women courted by dashing young men from out of town who made promises, to both them and their parents, of a wonderful future together. Young women at ice cream parlors, railway depots, fruit stores … the accounts reveal stunningly similar tactics and methods used by traffickers today. Even in the 1900s, the network was methodical and organized.

But then people rose up to try saving these young women. The crusaders were judges, prosecutors, missionaries, suffragettes, police captains, politicians, pastors, charity groups, and other individual activists who wanted to stop the deception and betrayal. At that time, sex trafficking was often referred to as the "white slave trade." Today, we understand the implications of that era and would put no emphasis on a particular ethnic group when seeking to save all exploited children.

Invariably, the media did what they could to sell papers, which drove public hysteria. But exaggeration wasn't necessary. The true stories were heartbreaking and often tragic, recounted by ministers and volunteers who went into the streets to find these young women, or by law enforcement, families whose daughters never returned, and the few girls rescued or able to escape, often returning home where they could never overcome their status as an immoral woman.

Some called it the greatest crime in the world's history.

However, more than 100 years later, American girls and boys are still being forced into sex slavery, sold to satisfy someone else's depravity. In this beautiful country of baseball and apple pie, the land of the free and home of the brave, it's stunning to discover that our children are being victimized in such a heinous manner. This is the underbelly of American culture that few people have known existed. For a long time, I was one of them.

The Mann Act of 1910

The crusaders of the early 1900s helped enforce the passage of The Mann Act of 1910. Signed by President Taft, The Mann Act made it a crime to transport women across state lines for the purpose of prostitution or debauchery, or any other immoral purpose. It was the first law in U.S. history to address trafficking in such a way.

Unfortunately, the wording of The Mann Act left room for abuses over the years. In 1913, it was used to prosecute a black boxer for riding with his white girlfriend across state lines. Charlie Chaplin and Chuck Berry were two famous personalities prosecuted erroneously under the intent of the Act as well. Consensual sexual relationships were prosecuted because of the "immoral purposes" wording of the Act. It took amendments in 1978 and 1986 to specifically apply the law to transportation across state lines for prostitution or illegal sexual acts.

Despite these instances, it is still a phenomenally useful law. Its passage marked the very first U.S. law to protect those we now call sex-trafficking victims. It gave law enforcement and prosecutors the ability to arrest pimps, whom we call traffickers today.

Yet, despite The Mann Act and its improvements, something happened and the momentum of this cause in America diminished. Along the way, the message was lost.

Just a few years after The Mann Act of 1910 passed, America would get pulled into the first World War. Next came the

Great Depression and World War II — changing the landscape and borders of nations all over the globe. Beginning in the '50s and extending into the '60s and '70s, America saw the Civil Rights Movement, the women's movement, the Korean War, the Vietnam War, and incredible cultural changes.

The voices calling out the injustice of trafficking victims dwindled to near silence.

And that is where this book begins.

In our world right now, there are regions and countries where humans are considered expendable. Governments brutalize their own citizens, hungry families sleep on the streets without hope for help, and children are considered commodities.

But the heart of America breaks when it hears about suffering. Our giving in charitable donations rivals all nations in the world. We have countless non-profits and religious groups whose mission is to help people. We are a nation of freedom fighters, a nation that cares. When we learn about the sexual victimization of innocent children — *any* child from *any* nation — there is no argument about right or wrong. There's no discussion over politics or whether it should or should not be stopped. We are enraged.

So why are American kids *still* being bought and sold for sex to predominantly American men? Why would this happen in a country that deeply cares about its children?

It has taken time for me to discover the complexities and depravities of the child sex-trafficking industry in America. Even while serving as a Congresswoman, and years into our work at Shared Hope International, I had no idea that children were being sold in the truck stops, motels, back alleys, and strip clubs of cities and towns across my beloved country, and even most recently through online facilitators. This was happening in the shadows beyond my initial sight. And it's still happening.

I've never been able to turn away from hurting women and children. While a Washington State Senator, I chaired the State Senate Children and Family Services Committee. In that role, I oversaw programs that focused on the protection and restoration of women and children — including adoption, child welfare, drug rehabilitation, and homeless child services. However, my first real introduction to sex trafficking didn't occur in the United States. That would remain hidden from me for years. It would be hidden from the other people you'll meet in this book as well.

My introduction came on a trip to Mumbai, India, that changed me forever. It began the journey that eventually unveiled what was happening right here, under our noses, in America.

In 1998, I was serving as United States Congresswoman of the 3rd Congressional District of the State of Washington. I lived in Vancouver, Washington, as I do now, where my other hats include wife, mother, and grandmother. My husband, Vern, and I were active in our church and have often had foster children in our home who'd come from troubled situations. The faces of children had kept me awake at night for years before this trip to India, but soon, my life would change profoundly because of the young women, kids, and especially one little girl I was about to encounter.

"I want you to see for yourself what is happening here," a missionary told me when he invited me to Mumbai. Mr. Grant had heard me speak at a General Council Meeting of the Assemblies

A 2010 United Nations Office on Drugs and Crime report estimates that globally 79% of identified victims of human trafficking were trafficked for sexual exploitation, 18% for forced labor, and 3% for other forms of exploitation.

of God Church and knew that we shared the belief that every person is uniquely made by God. India would be a research trip to experience what I'd been hearing about when it came to international sex slavery.

I wonder if this is how the crusaders of the early 1900s spread their message, by asking another person to come see what was happening? It most certainly worked for me.

During the daytime, the streets in Mumbai were crowded with people, tuk tuks, motorcycles, and vehicles. My nose was filled with the smell of diesel from the traffic, incense and curry wafting from buildings and outdoor stalls, and, at times, a whiff of garbage. As night fell, Falkland Road's cloak was ripped away — the truth revealed.

I walked down that road with a small group including K.K. Devaraj, the founder of Bombay Teen Challenge, and my friend Susan. I wanted to cover my mouth and nose from the stench of sewage along the gutters of the street, but I clenched my teeth and kept my face from showing the emotions surging inside. Women and girls looked out from windows or stared from between the bars of bottom-story windows. In the background, I could see their owners watching over their human products.

Quite a few of these young girls were from Nepal, more than a thousand miles away, where their families had sold them to traffickers or had been tricked into believing their daughters were being given a great opportunity to work in a carpet factory or as a house servant and would be sending money back home to the family. Instead, the girls were brought to the brothels and forced into the sex trade. They were told they owed enormous debts for their travel, clothing, and housing. Once they "worked off" their debt they'd be allowed to leave. The debts were often too large to ever be paid off, or they were continually added to. Pimps also used threats of torture or death against their families to keep them in slavery, often for the rest of their short lives.

Others were girls from villages in India and brought here under similar situations. Because of the cultural caste system of the country, these girls were considered less valuable. I would later learn that in every country, and even in the United States, it is this devaluation of (certain) human lives that allows the sex industry to exist.

As I walked, my eyes connected with the dark eyes of one small girl in an alleyway. I was drawn toward the child — she couldn't have been older than my then 11-year-old granddaughter.

I knew this child had no hope. There was no comfort to be found in this place. Then I felt as if God whispered straight into my heart: *Touch her, for me.*

The child's hair was likely lice infested, and her clothes hung on her fragile body, dirty and torn. I knew this girl had seen and experienced more in her few years of life than most adults would ever have to know.

As I embraced this girl on the street, my life was reshaped. Today I can still feel her little body in my arms. I remember the beat of her heart against my own.

I knew then that I had to do something.

Linda married Vern in 1968, shortly before turning 18, and they raised two children. Vern has been an integral part of SHI's journey from the very beginning.

I flew home and poured out every story and emotion to my husband, Vern, and then after him to every friend and colleague I encountered. I couldn't stop telling people about what I had witnessed. Politics was not my future, at least, not in the role I'd been serving, I was sure. Soon after, I launched Shared Hope International (SHI).

Starting Shared Hope felt as if everything I'd done in the past had equipped me for this — my true calling. I knew about policy and how to stand my ground in D.C. when fighting for social needs in government, sometimes even against my own party and against political advice. My supporters and friends — once dubbed "Linda's Army" — were people with conviction and honor. I didn't doubt that they would take up this cause once they heard about it. Later, I would realize that without these people launching the write-in campaign in 1994 that brought me to Congress, I wouldn't have gone to India, nor ever witnessed the tragic reality that inspired me to found Shared Hope. They were the impetus for much more than an elected seat. Unconnected pieces kept coming together until the puzzle of Shared Hope fit.

Once I started Shared Hope and had a board of ardent believers like me, we dove in to focus on those women and girls in India and Nepal. We worked with local leaders to build two villages in less than three years, and they soon began to fill them with women from the safe houses or new ones fleeing the brothels.

I called upon every friendship and political connection to help wake the world up even as I was awakening to the vast and complex world of human trafficking around the globe. As passionate as I was, nothing prepared me for what I would learn in the years to come. I knew pieces of the issue, but the scale was staggering. There was no clear path forward. So much was unchartered in this battleground. I needed to find others who had knowledge and were out there working to change the world — others who were kept awake at night thinking of all the lost souls out there … who heard the cries of women and children in their dreams and felt the tugs on their hearts while seeking a way to help.

This was a time when connectivity was much more limited. Media hadn't saturated our lives at home, at work, in entertainment. Stories and opinions are now shared on social media in real time and in a constant flow. A leader can tweet to millions of followers, and crowd-funding on a mobile device has become commonplace and often oversaturated.

But this was the late '90s. People were just starting to embrace text messaging and using dial-up Internet in widening mediums. Groups fighting injustice had no efficient way to

In 1994, Linda Smith was elected to U.S. Congress after a write-in campaign put together by a grassroots group of supporters with diverse political views. She served as a U.S. Congresswoman from 1995-1999.

connect or communicate to share resources and knowledge. These groups, non-profits, and individuals were often single pins of light drawn together for a conference or a seminar and then sent off to their corners of the globe to battle it out again. But if we could unite, I knew we could turn the tide.

Shared Hope International needed to bridge the divisions and connect the gaps, especially for those who were already working to end sex trafficking. Even as Shared Hope's work began — and I became immersed in our strategy to prevent sex trafficking, bring justice to victims, and help survivors in their process of restoration — I was missing something essential. Something that made my blood run cold. The fact that child trafficking was happening in our own neighborhoods. I had a global view, not realizing there was a domestic issue thriving beneath my sight.

As Shared Hope International built safe-haven villages for girls in India, Nepal, South Africa, and Fiji, connected with the U.S. Department of State to host events around the world, worked to change laws, and put together training materials, there were girls right on the streets of Vancouver, Washington, and across the bridge in Portland, Oregon, whose cries finally reached my ears.

Our children had been crying for some time, and America couldn't hear them. In 1910, people were waking up to the issue, but, for whatever reason, a dark veil had since clouded it.

In the late 1990s and early 2000s, most of us thought sex trafficking was an international issue. As we discovered it through our research, I had to wonder: When and how did this begin in the United States? I'd find that from colonial days and through the Gold Rush and expansion, all the way to modern-day, this underbelly of American culture has been filled with the cries of victimized children. It has often been camouflaged with the name of "prostitution" to create the idea that these young women and children are complicit, as if they are responsible individuals who chose such a life to benefit themselves. But what could a child gain from such heinous victimization? What woman thrives under the real-life conditions of sex slavery (not the Hollywood version) that include abuse, disease, and the forfeiture of self-worth, love, family, and dignity?

The history of women forced into sex trafficking is one of heartache, desperation, and loss … and often starts with former childhood abuse. Brothels have never housed joy, independence, and love. For children, there is never a choice involved in prostitution. Their victimization cannot be self-motivated — it is fueled by money and greed and financed through lust.

Those crusaders of the early 1900s saw the issue. They did not see the end of it as they'd hoped, but they did get a good law, The Mann Act, passed with their efforts. And now, I want to introduce you to some modern crusaders. Most of them, like me, came into the issue of domestic minor sex trafficking by accident. There are many other names and voices of brave men and women in the fight against sex trafficking. I have included just a few of the many in this book. These individuals, with different personalities, backgrounds, and life and career directions, have made unique contributions to the effort to end the sex trafficking of America's youth.

Many people seek a singular calling or purpose in life, but I've seen how a life mission can evolve and change through the course of living it out. The people I'll introduce you to often had no plans to be part of the battle against child sex trafficking, but once they discovered what was happening, they couldn't turn away. I want these people to become your people. If you're willing, I want to show you where we came from and where we are going.

These battle-worn freedom fighters have greatly influenced me. Together and apart, we have made great advances. I cannot share every individual, non-governmental organization, or ministry group who has made an impact, but those who do follow represent many unsung heroes, and the even more heroic voices of survivors who seek to rebuild their lives.

I'm here to tell you: There's a dark secret in America that has finally been revealed. Now that we are seeing it and listening, it's time to share what we know — that this injustice of sexually trafficked children must be stopped.

The progress should be revisited. The steps behind can inspire our onward battles. First, we'll look back at our modern crusade, and then we'll look ahead.

In 2014, there were 466,949 entries regarding missing children (younger than 18) by law enforcement agencies.[1]

There is an enormous amount of work yet to accomplish, and we need your help to do it. As we've discovered, when individuals stand together against the Goliaths of this world, miracles are possible.

"For God's sake, do something!"

That's our battle cry today. For nearly 20 years, I've been involved in *doing something*, as have the people you're about to meet.

But we can do more than something; we can change our world.

---

[1]"FAQS: Missing Children." National Center for Missing and Exploited Children, http://www. missingkids.com/theissues/missing.

2

THE KNOCK ON HIS OFFICE DOOR

Ernie Allen

> **"IT WOULD BE THE SEED OF SOMETHING THAT WOULD CHANGE CULTURE, SHAPE PROCEDURES IN LAW ENFORCEMENT, AND SAVE COUNTLESS LIVES. RIGHT NOW, IT WAS NARROWED IN ON LOUISVILLE, KENTUCKY. THE STEPS FORWARD WOULD WIDEN AND FAN OUT UNTIL IT WOULD EVENTUALLY SCALE THE GLOBE.**
>
> **BUT FIRST, THERE WERE THE MURDERS."**
>
> **ERNIE ALLEN**

Two decades before and thousands of miles away from where I walked along Falkland Road in India, a young attorney named Ernie Allen was about to take his first step into a new vision. And it all began with a knock on his office door. But I'll let Ernie tell his story …

***

In 1978, when I was the Director of the Louisville-Jefferson County Crime Commission in Louisville, Kentucky, the trajectory of my focus was changed by a knock on my office door.

I was pulled away from the usual issues of the day when I heard the knock and welcomed two men into my office.

"John," I said, reaching for the first man's hand, and then the other. "Professor Rice. This is a surprise."

John Rabun was a social worker in charge of managing the county's group homes. Professor J. Kerry Rice was a professor at the University of Louisville. We had met when John was earning his master's degree from the Kent School of Social Work where Professor Rice taught. I knew the men had become friends after discussing local concerns. Together, they'd begun weighing out changes that might make some effective contributions in their community. What I didn't know was what had brought them to my office that day.

A group home is licensed differently in every state. It often refers to a place in which children and youth of the foster care system are placed until foster families are found for them. Unrelated children live in a home-like setting with either a set of house parents or a rotating staff of trained caregivers.

The men were friendly, but the stiff formality and expressions on their faces alerted me that this was no social visit. I offered them a seat. Small talk was short — after all, we were all busy professionals.

"We have a serious problem in the community, and we need you to help," John started.

"What is this serious problem?" I asked. Every day, I tackled problems in the community — crime problems — and these guys did too. This had to be serious to bring them both in to see me.

"We've got kids disappearing from our county group homes and no one is paying attention."

I leaned forward and listened.

The two men explained their joint concern for these kids. They'd driven the streets looking for them since no one else seemed to care about or know their fate. There were huge gaps and chasms in the juvenile justice system. The group homes couldn't find them, and they weren't looking. They'd notified social services, but that agency was overwhelmed with cases. These kids were "just runaways" and no longer on the social services radar. The children didn't have families checking in, so no one was reporting them missing. No one was looking, nobody cared.

"So where are they then?" I asked.

John and Professor Rice explained how they weren't disappearing off the face of the earth. They weren't hanging out on the beach in California. They hadn't "run away" very far.

"They're still here," Professor Rice said.

"So we have a runaway problem? Homeless situation?" I asked, thinking through what agencies should be involved. Here were two professionals coming to my office to have a conversation about runaways from a group home? I wasn't sure I fully understood.

"They aren't just running away," Professor Rice explained. "They're being lured away by pimps pretending to be their boyfriends. Eventually, they get arrested for prostitution and end up in juvenile hall or they're released back to the pimps.

"These aren't bad kids. The pimps and system are making them bad. First they come from awful family situations and are sent to the group homes. Then they're lured from there and basically forced into prostitution, where they're arrested and turned into criminals.

"When they're arrested, law enforcement doesn't realize where they're from. Social services isn't informing the police since they are categorized as runaways, and so they're falling through the cracks because no one is communicating."

The men explained further. The system was failing because the agencies were silos. In the school system, educators were teaching and interacting with kids. They saw children in trouble, but there were no avenues to connect with them. Mental health providers served the mentally ill brought to their hospitals, but there was no connection outside of the institution. Social services had its duties, and the police did what police were supposed to do.

These kids transcended the system. They were being victimized in horrendous ways, prostituted out on the streets, and the systems and agencies designed to protect them were failing miserably.

"And you two have an idea on how to solve this?" I asked.

"We have some ideas," John Rabun said. "But we need you to make them happen."

The three of us brainstormed the rest of the day. That meeting was the launching pad for a new approach that bridged traditional barriers between social services and law enforcement.

In the city of Louisville, there were police services, but no social services. That was a county agency governed by county government.

The three of us agreed the first plan of action was to go to the county judge. Soon a task force was formed. It didn't seem like much at the time, but it was one of those moments that gained significance looking back.

In that moment, a nerve was struck — that this was important to me — but it would be later that I'd realize how momentous this discussion was for my future *and* the futures of untold other people across the country. It would be the seed of something that would change culture, shape procedures in law enforcement, and save countless lives. Right now, it was narrowed in on Louisville, Kentucky. The steps forward would widen and fan out until it would eventually scale the globe.

But first, there were the murders.

3

A Victim's Story

This is Jimmy's Story. Jimmy is a fictionalized character based on an unidentified victim of the John Wayne Gacy murders. He was most likely killed in August 1976, after being picked up from Clark Street in Chicago, Illinois.

At the age of 14, "Jimmy" knew well the Chicagoan streets of the Chicken Hawk district. He'd been out there over a year, and he believed he'd seen it all and could handle anything.

On this cool August night, he leaned against the side of a brick building smoking a cigarette, talking to two of the young women out working with him. Lisa was an older prostitute and sometimes treated him like her favorite little brother, ruffling his hair and calling him "Hon." Milly was a new girl, and Jimmy had been trying to figure how to teach her some street smarts. The older girls kept applying more makeup to cover Milly's bruises and the dark circles under her eyes. She needed to adapt and wise up like he'd learned to do.

Jimmy pulled his jacket tighter around him. Even though it was early August, it was a cool night. Sometimes he thought about living on a farm. He remembered the smell of the corn fields, the taste of fresh milk, a younger childhood catching frogs and playing with the calves and lambs. He'd had a dog who loved him more than probably anyone else in the entire world, and if that dog were still alive, Jimmy wouldn't have been able to leave him behind. But every good memory led back to the bad. As awful as it was on the streets, for all the deplorable deeds he'd been required to perform, there was something worse about being beaten and mistreated by someone you loved and who was supposed to love you. Out here, Jimmy knew the rules and what was expected. Back home, he could never figure out his papa's rages.

Jimmy dropped the butt of his cigarette, smashing it against the sidewalk with his tennis shoe. He reached for the pack of Marlboro Reds in his back pocket and laughed at something Lisa said, though he'd barely been listening. A black sedan came slowly down Clark Street toward them, the sure sign of someone cruising. It slowed further, so Jimmy and Lisa walked to the edge of the sidewalk, with Milly coming up behind.

"It's for you," Lisa said to him, stepping back. The car had stopped, and the middle-aged man stared at only one of them. The man rolled down the window, and Jimmy leaned inside. It was warm and smelled of aftershave. The guy asked if he wanted to party, and, of course, Jimmy said that he did. The guy seemed okay enough, unlike some who made Jimmy want to run the opposite direction (and on a few occasions, he did just that).

"See you guys in a bit," Jimmy said as he opened the car door. He gave Milly a wave and then an exaggerated wink to get a smile out of her. The poor kid looked both relieved and terrified that he was the one being picked up.

Jimmy rode away in the sedan, but he would never return to Clark Street. Two and a half years later, his body was found buried in the crawl space of a suburban house along with dozens of other boys and young men.

No one was looking for Jimmy. He'd never be identified. No one would ever know his story. He might have grown up on a farm, or he may never have seen a cow and corn field in person at all. Whatever his past, there was not one pleasant reason that landed him on Clark Street.

Maybe a grandparent, a cousin, a former classmate, or one of the young women he'd known on the streets might have wondered, "Whatever happened to Jimmy?"

But other than that, Jimmy was forgotten — his grave forever unnamed.

1972-1978

At least 33 teenage boys and young men were sexually assaulted, tortured, and murdered by John Wayne Gacy between 1972 and 1978.

Seven victims were never identified.

One survivor who escaped Gacy's house recalled how Gacy and another man drugged him and, together, sexually assaulted and tortured him. Such behavior is not uncommon for pedophiles who enjoy bragging about their acts and desiring others to experience them. It was never proven that Gacy had accomplices in his killings. The other victims did not live to tell their stories.

Invading the Darkness

4

Missing Kids in America

Ernie Allen

> "THESE TRUSTED CUSTOMERS COULD PURCHASE A CHILD FOR SEX. AND YOU KNOW WHAT? THEY COULD EVEN USE THEIR CREDIT CARDS FOR PAYMENT ... AFTER THE TRANSACTION, THE SERVICE INCLUDED DELIVERY OF THE CHILD TO THE PURCHASER. THE PURCHASER COULD USE THE CHILD FOR A PREDETERMINED AMOUNT OF TIME, THEN THE KID WAS PICKED UP AND RETURNED TO THE LOCATION WHERE CHILDREN WERE BEING HELD. THEY WERE BEING SOLD AGAIN, AND AGAIN."
>
> **ERNIE ALLEN**

Ernie's life changed direction yet again in 1978, when a friendly man who ran a construction company was revealed as a serial killer. As he began to discover more, it would be the missing children of America who called Ernie to a life and fight he never expected …

***

I was on a business trip to Chicago when the John Wayne

Gacy murders broke.

I'd come to the city with Ron Pregliasco and Bill Bardenwerper from the Louisville crime commission and county services to review Chicago's new 9-1-1 system. The national emergency number for the United States was slowly spreading from city to city across the country, and we'd come to see how it worked and what it might cost to implement back in Louisville.

But that cold winter, the news was flooded by a shocking discovery. In a Chicago suburb, John Wayne Gacy, a respected local businessman and frequent clown performer at children's parties, had been hiding a horrific secret. Law enforcement was uncovering body after body from beneath Gacy's crawl space, garage floor, and even feet from his outdoor grill.

Thirty-three bodies of young men, many under 18, were being pulled from his suburban home. He had been raping, torturing, and murdering boys and young men for a decade.

My colleagues and I were as shocked, along with the entire country. Ever since the conversation months earlier with Professor Rice and John Rabun, I'd been thinking about all the disconnects and crimes we might be overlooking. The three of us had been moved into action after that meeting. A task force was created and we had been working to bridge agencies in our city. But this Gacy news nagged at me. How could so many missing young men have gone unnoticed in a place as modern as Chicago? It wasn't a criticism, but rather a fear — if we'd been unaware of the issues with runaways and prostituted kids in Louisville, what else might be happening beyond our sight? Chicago law enforcement was as good as any, so what had gone wrong, and what if we had a similar problem?

MISSING KIDS IN AMERICA

I knew Chicago's law enforcement was overrun and overwhelmed with those murders. The media wanted answers, broken-hearted parents sought to know if their sons were among the dead, and the shock of so many murdered in one location had created panic in the area. Forensic teams were still digging out bodies, detectives were gathering evidence for Gacy's eventual trial. I needed to get back to Louisville, but I couldn't pass up this opportunity to get some information, so I contacted the superintendent of the Chicago Police Department.

I explained who I was and what Ron and Bill and I hoped to gain. "We've been working on crimes against children in Kentucky and just happen to be in Chicago right now to view the new 9-1-1 system. I hoped we might meet with the officers assigned to the Gacy case."

The superintendent was polite, but unsure. "You're welcome to it as long as the commander and officers are on board."

It wasn't long and I had permission. Since the three of us had to get back to Louisville soon, the commander agreed for us to do a ride-along during the 11 p.m. to 7 a.m. shift. We showed up and met with the police officers who had been part of the Gacy case and knew details not released to the public. The medical examiner and detectives were still trying to identify bodies, and they feared some of the victims might never be known. Gacy had targeted some young men and boys through his construction company, or with a friendly invitation to his house, but other victims had been runaways or boys in forced-prostitution rings.

We loaded up with the officers and drove to the side of Chicago where Gacy had confessed to picking up many of his victims. We drove along Clark and Rush Streets in what was called the Chicken Hawk district. It was a cold winter, in the middle of the night, but I saw clearly what was being offered as they stood in the cold along the street. A few cars with lone male drivers cruised up and down — the young women and young men would approach the vehicles as they slowed. When they saw us, they turned away from the curb as our police cruiser passed, but I caught just how young many of them were. And it surprised me that this business was all out in the open.

I knew that Louisville had its own dark side too. If Gacy could happen here in Chicago, what was stopping someone similar from doing this in Kentucky? Maybe nothing ...

The officers told us that on numerous occasions, Gacy's name had come up in investigations of missing young men in the area. Some who were found dead had worked for his construction company or were last seen going to talk about a potential job. One set of parents had been certain that Gacy was involved in their son's disappearance, but no one had listened seriously enough until now.

Then it was discovered that Gacy had served time in another state for sodomy of a minor, but law enforcement in Chicago didn't know about that until after his arrest. Again, no good system was in place so that information like that could be shared with different city and county agencies. Gacy had behaved like an upstanding citizen in public; he was a father and had been married. But very little alluded to the fact that he'd been picking up street kids and killing them for years. No one had put it together until three dozen were dead.

We returned to the station house as morning broke over the city. One of the officers remarked about another astonishing case we might be interested in.

"We arrested this John Norman who was running a child pornography business, but for his most trusted customers, he had another service available. A very discrete service."

I had a feeling I knew what that service was, but waited to hear about it.

"These trusted customers could purchase a child for sex. And you know what? They could even use their credit cards for payment."

"Credit cards? You've got to be kidding me," I said astounded. Credit cards in 1979 needed a bulky table-top device

> Before the computerization of credit card systems in America, using a credit card to pay at a merchant was significantly more complicated than it is today. It was common at this time for merchants to accept charges without first verifying the credit limit over the phone.

with a carbon sheet between the merchant copy and the customer's receipt. People didn't use credit cards for daily purchases at that time, and so the idea that they'd pay for sex with a child using a credit card was ludicrous.

"After the transaction, the service included delivery of the child to the purchaser. The purchaser could use the child for a predetermined amount of time, then the kid was picked up and returned to the location where the children were being held. They were being sold again, and again."

My stomach churned as I listened to this. Where were these kids now, and how long had this been going on? John Norman's child sex-trafficking ring was called the *Delta Project*. Like Gacy, Norman had been arrested before, in Dallas, but then he'd fled to Chicago and set up shop once again. The officer told me how Norman had kept careful records of his clients on neatly written and organized cards that included the names and addresses of these buyers.

"You have the list of these customers?"

"We do. Before you head home, do you want the names of Norman's clients from Kentucky?" the officer asked me.

I blinked at this. Kentucky was two states away, and yet there were cards from men in my home state who were part of this trusted clientele in Chicago?

"Most certainly I would. I'll take the cards to our guys back home," I said quickly, feeling a drive for justice rise within me. This was certainly unexpected, but also a great lead toward catching predators back home and potentially saving some kids.

I followed the officer to a Xerox machine there in the police department. We ended up spending the entire day making copies of the names of John Norman's Kentucky customers. Copy after copy, the weight of it hung heavy on my shoulders. I thought of those decomposing bodies being pulled from beneath Gacy's house … of the parents trying to get answers for their missing boys … of the bodies of the kids no one was looking for. I couldn't decide what was worse — the anguish of parents or the tragedy of unloved murdered boys who might never be named or known.

"That's it for Kentucky," the officer finally said. I looked at the other names and states we hadn't copied. It was 7:30 p.m. We had copied 500 names.

The problem wasn't only in Chicago. It was back home in Kentucky and across the entire country as well. I heard a police commander say, "The only way not to find this problem in your city is to simply not look."

My colleagues and I, from that moment, set out to look.

I carried those copies of 500 cards back to Louisville and took them to the Office of the Jefferson County Executive to see Judge Mitch McConnell (later a senior U.S. Senator and Senate Majority Leader).

I dropped the stack of Xeroxed cards onto Judge McConnell's desk and began talking about Chicago, Clark Street and the Chicken Hawk district, Gacy, and the Delta Project with its buy-and-sell-kids-with-credit-cards business model.

"The only reason we aren't digging up bodies in some cellar in Louisville is that by the grace of God, when Gacy got out of prison in Iowa, he moved to Chicago," I said. "He just settled right in there as a businessman and trusted member of the community. If he'd moved to Louisville, I don't believe we could have stopped him."

Judge McConnell listened to everything I'd discovered and flipped through the sheets of paper. About half of the 500 names lived in the Louisville area — the other half spread across Kentucky. The cards on the judge's desk were an ominous image of what criminals were hiding right under our noses.

He was clearly shaken by the information. The Gacy case was national news, and more and more horrific details were being revealed.

"I have some suggestions," I stated, and I told him about the meeting with John Rabun and Professor Rice, and how we'd been pulling together county agencies to work together.

"We need something broader now," I said.

Judge McConnell was a man of action, and my suggestion moved him to act immediately. After that meeting, he created a multi-agency investigative task force to evaluate the community, and he asked me to chair it. The task force included prosecutors, social workers, postal inspectors, and the FBI, as well as city, county, and state police.

1979

The formation of this multi-agency investigative task force in Louisville, KY, was the first of its kind to bring city and county agencies together to collaborate information for solving crimes and obtaining prosecutions.

We were all motivated to make this work. Soon, agencies crossed duties and information with one another.

Initially we focused on the most vulnerable in their communities — kids being sexually exploited. Police rode with social workers and followed up on children who'd gone missing from group homes and foster care. Social workers rode with police and saw the streets where kids were being sold. Prosecutors explained to law enforcement what they needed to prosecute perpetrators. Where once agencies were islands, generally speaking, doing their own work, now information was being shared and coordinated among them.

I was relieved when our task force could find no evidence of a Gacy-type tragedy in Louisville. We didn't have enough missing kids to fit the profile of a serial killer in our midst. However, we did confirm that child victimization was a serious problem in the city of Louisville and Jefferson County, and that local government agencies and community leaders had missed it.

It wasn't a ground-breaking, complex plan. It was common-sense, really. The task force helped connect people so that someone was following up, communicating data and ideas, and taking the time to track down missing kids.

And it had immediate results. Children were rescued and perpetrators arrested.

For the next step, the Louisville-Jefferson County Exploited and Missing Child Unit (EMCU) was created. John Rabun was designated to serve as the Manager of the Unit by Judge McConnell. I chaired the task force and the new Unit was

PRIOR TO 1980

When a child went missing before 1980, there were no Amber Alerts, no hotlines, no collaboration between agencies or police departments.

9-1-1 systems were just beginning to be implemented.

Parents of missing kids were left disconnected, and without many resources — often asking for the rest of their lives, "What happened to my child?"

based in my office at the Crime Commission. Similarly, all members of the Unit, including city and county police, county social workers, prosecutors, and a few others, were detailed to my office to work as a part of this new group.

Now we had a single entity focused on kids who were being victimized or had disappeared in the area. The task force kept the agencies working together, and now information could go directly to one source.

Simultaneously, the media heard about our efforts. Stories of the busts spread, and reporters showed up to find out what was happening. It began with local media coverage and quickly went state-wide, and then nationally.

Sometimes I'd think of those other index cards I hadn't taken back to Kentucky. What about those men in other states who were buying children for sex? And what about those kids? Given the immediate success of the EMCU, I knew such a program was needed everywhere — the country over.

Late in 1979, I contacted the U.S. Department of Justice and proposed a summit on missing and exploited children. The country needed a national strategy with a missing children's registry and a fund that would help create specialty units, like task forces in cities and towns across the United States. I received a polite-enough reply from the Justice Department — nothing was going to happen.

Then murders started happening in Atlanta.

The killings began mid-1979, and, by 1980, bodies were being discovered month after month. Most were African-American children, some young adults. Each new victim found meant the panic grew. News of the "Atlanta Child Murders," as they were being called, swept America. The story was featured on the front page of national newspapers and became the lead story on network news nationwide, and then worldwide. Twenty-six African-American children had gone missing, one after the other, and soon after were found murdered.

An Atlanta television crew flew to Louisville to film a story about our task force and how our efforts were working in the community. We welcomed the media with hopes that it would help other areas and children beyond our borders. But when the story aired, the focus wasn't about one community's attempt to stop the victimization of children ... instead it became a criticism of the Atlanta Police Department and their response to the murders. The public was in a panic — everyone wanted *someone* to blame. The message expressed over the featured segment was that if Atlanta had something like our Louisville task force, maybe these children wouldn't be dead.

This obviously wasn't helpful to Atlanta's police departments — and it didn't endear them to our task force either. But an Atlanta-based friend of mine, Dr. Ozell Sutton, served as Regional Director of the Justice Department's Community Relations Service. Dr. Sutton and I had worked together in the past. After the story aired, he went to the U.S. Justice Department and persuaded them to invite John Rabun and me to Atlanta to consult on the child murders.

John and I went immediately.

Our first job was to overcome any rift caused by the media. We met with top police officials and made it clear we were there to help, not to run the investigation nor conduct any media interviews. Our purpose was solely to help.

I explained that our task force and EMCU were new entities formed because of what I'd seen in Chicago. We were there to share what we'd learned, that was all.

Atlanta police were skeptical at first, but they were also overwhelmed with the mounting pressure. Speculations were running wild. People feared this might be some KKK organization out killing African-American kids. Were these deaths a hate crime or the acts of a serial killer? Children were dead, and they didn't know who was behind it.

I asked the officers to identify locations around the city, like Clark Street in Chicago. Every city had a strip or area in the community where prostitution and drugs were prevalent — that location would also include children being victimized.

It only took about 10 minutes to find it once we headed out, but I was shocked. The "red light district" was huge. Though the children being killed in Atlanta weren't kids being sold on the streets, I knew that most predators had some connections that could be traced back to places like this.

Once John and I had a clearer idea of what was happening there, we went to work sharing the processes, mistakes, and what had worked for us in Louisville — information that could transcend this case and bring changes needed for other cases as well. It was a nationwide problem I was convinced could only be solved with support from Washington, D.C.

At this same time, Vice President George H.W. Bush flew to Atlanta as a representative of President Ronald Reagan and the federal government. They wanted to show their commitment to stopping this horrific tragedy.

I knew this was my chance.

When I had a moment, I told the Vice President that what we were seeing in Atlanta wasn't just happening in Atlanta.

"This isn't about one city, or one serial murder case. It is happening in communities across this country, and America has missed it."

Vice President Bush was listening. As a result, I sent a formal proposal to the Vice President that included a White House Conference on Missing and Exploited Children.

After our work in Atlanta was done, I returned to my family and office in Louisville. It wasn't long before I heard back from D.C. They were sympathetic to the problems and issues. They weren't turning away from it, and said the ideas were great. But the White

House conference I proposed would be expensive, and the budget was tight. It just wasn't a possibility at that time. The final word was, "Don't let this stop you. Go ahead and do it yourself."

I met the task force in Louisville, and we were all in agreement: "Okay, let's do it."

The *Child Tragedies National Symposium on Exploited and Victimized Children* was held at the Hyatt in Louisville in early December 1981. It brought together a cross-section of experts from numerous backgrounds with the goal of developing a national strategy.

Among the speakers were Lee Brown, the Public Safety Commissioner who oversaw the Atlanta Child Murders; Jefferson County Judge McConnell; Gilbert Pompa, who served as Director of Community Relations Service from the Justice Department; Kenneth Wooden, an investigative reporter, Director of the National Coalition for Children's Justice, and author of *Weeping in the Playtime of Others*, a piece that chronicled what he called the "staggering" abuses he'd discovered against incarcerated children in the United States. There were members of Congress, law enforcement, judges,

From July 1980 to February 1984, the police/social work team of the Louisville-Jefferson County Exploited and Missing Child Unit (EMCU) investigated approximately 1,400 cases of children suspected of being victims of sexual exploitation. A full 54% (756) of the children were found to be victims, and the EMCU prosecuted hundreds of adults for various crimes involving the sexual exploitation of children.

More than 40 major cases resulted in the successful prosecution of adults involved with more than 12 children each.[1]

attorneys, and representatives of social services.

And then there were the parents.

The parents came not because of their professions or desire for social change, but instead because they had experienced the greatest horror a person could encounter.

Julie and Stanley Patz's six-year-old, Etan Patz, was still missing after he had disappeared two years earlier while on his way to his bus stop in New York.

John and Reve Walsh had lost their six-year-old son, Adam, only the summer before. He was kidnapped from a mall in Florida and found murdered weeks later. While searching for their boy, the Walshes were stunned by the lack of coordination between law enforcement agencies even within their own state. How were missing kids to be found when police a city away weren't even aware or looking?

After his son's murder, John Walsh dedicated his life to hunting criminals and to helping find missing children. He became a criminal investigator, human and victim rights advocate, and host and creator of TV shows focused on solving missing person cases and catching offenders, including *America's Most Wanted* and *The Hunt with John Walsh.*

John and his wife, Reve, are cofounders in the National Center for Missing and Exploited Children.

Camille Bell was the mother of a young victim in the Atlanta Child Murders. She spoke about how the nation had focused on the mass murders in Atlanta and after Gacy in Chicago, but then that essentially everyone went back to sleep. She was determined to keep America awake.

Rosemary Kohm's 11-year-old daughter had been found murdered in April in the rural town of Santa Claus, Indiana. It was said that if such a crime could happen in little Santa Claus, it could happen anywhere.

Despite the grief of these parents, they were doggedly determined to see changes implemented.

This was a time when police could enter stolen cars, guns, and even horses into the FBI's crime database, but they couldn't enter the names of missing kids. The FBI said there were too many missing children, and it would clog up their system.

That was no longer an acceptable response.

The country had 50 states that acted individually — much like the initial problem in Louisville we'd sought to solve, bringing different departments, services, and organizations to work together. Across the country, the states were doing the same but on a macro level. There were 18,000 police departments nationwide that rarely communicated with one another, let alone anything on a cohesive national level.

I remember someone stating what we all felt: "We can't just let this be a conference where we get worked up and talk about the problems. Let's get something done."

We paused from the schedule and came together to create a 23-Point Action Agenda. Two of the most critical points were 1) to enact a federal law requiring the sharing of information regarding missing kids, and 2) to create a national resource center that focused solely on missing and exploited children.

The symposium ended with solid plans to implement our 23 points. The media presence throughout was one of the most successful pieces of the conference in getting information out. Ned Potter of *ABC News* aired stories every night, and state and national papers wrote about the pleas of the parents to the world. Missing kids was an issue whose time had come. The news provided a way for these parents to communicate their pain across the country, and our group offered solutions now that we had the public's attention.

I'd always seen the idea of a national center as an obvious arm of the Justice Department or the FBI. Then I heard that President Reagan wasn't ignoring the issue or passing the buck. When VP Bush said they wanted to give support, he'd meant it despite the initial outcome of my proposal for a White House Summit.

President Reagan liked the idea of a national center too, but he didn't believe it should be a government entity. He believed it should be a private organization that had public support. This way, the center would remain autonomous of government bureaucracy, but it could also receive grants and support from the federal government.

On June 13, 1984, the National Center for Missing and Exploited Children was born. Founders included John and Reve Walsh, John Rabun, and others. I was honored to serve as

---

1982, 1984

The Missing Children Act of 1982 authorized the FBI to enter information about missing children into the National Crime Information Center. Law enforcement was then able to access this information to assist in finding missing kids.

The Missing Children's Assistance Act of 1984 provided the first free national hotline for missing kids and established a national resource center and clearinghouse to: (1) provide technical assistance to state and local governments and agencies in locating missing children; (2) coordinate public and private efforts to recover missing children; (3) disseminate information on innovative missing children's programs, services, and legislation; and (4) provide technical assistance to law enforcement agencies, state

Founding Chairman. An official ceremony was held in the East Room of the White House.

Soon I found myself saying good-bye to my beloved Kentucky and moving to Washington, D.C., where I'd serve as President/CEO of NCMEC. I told my wife we'd live in D.C. for only five years.

The Missing Children Act had passed in 1982. The Missing Children's Assistance Act was passed in 1984, and the national 24-hour toll-free missing children's hotline (1-800-THE-LOST) was established.

For missing children, nationwide changes had finally begun. I was proud of the work. Before I knew it, a decade passed with children being saved and new processes implemented nationwide. My wife supported the stay, even if she missed Louisville as much as I did.

When I heard about what Linda Smith and Shared

and local governments, and public and private nonprofit agencies.

The Act requires the Administrator to publish an annual summary of research on missing children and prepare a comprehensive plan for coordinating activities of all agencies and organizations responsible for missing children.

It authorizes the Administrator to make grants for research or demonstration or service programs designed to: (1) educate parents and community agencies on ways to prevent the abduction or sexual exploitation of children; (2) assist in the recovery or tracking of missing children; (3) aid communities in collecting material to assist parents in the identification of their children; (4) demonstrate the psychological consequences of a child's abduction; and (5) collect data on investigative practices utilized by law enforcement agencies.[2]

Ernie Allen was instrumental in bringing technology and innovation to the Center for Missing and Exploited Children. He appeared on *Oprah, The Today Show, Good Morning America, Larry King Live,* and many others to spread the word about America's missing children.

In May 1990, the U.S. Department of Justice released a study reporting that in 1988 there were as many as:

- 114,600 attempted abductions of children by nonfamily members

- 4,600 abductions by nonfamily members reported to police

- 300 abductions by nonfamily members where the children were gone for long periods of time or were murdered

- 354,000 children abducted by family members

- 450,700 children who ran away

- 127,100 children who were thrown away

- 438,200 children who were lost, injured, or otherwise missing[3]

Hope International were focused on, I felt drawn back to my beginnings in Louisville. The National Center for Missing and Exploited Children had focused our energy mainly on the "missing" part of our name, not the "exploited." But I was drawn first into child issues because of sexual exploitation — those group home kids who'd gone missing.

When I met with Linda and the subject of missing kids came up, I told her, "I know where the kids are. I've been saying it for years."

We'd been waking up the nation about missing kids. Now it was time to wake them up about children and sex trafficking in the United States.

[1] "Child Molesters: A behavioral analysis." National Center for Missing and Exploited Children in cooperation with the FBI. page v. https://www.ncjrs.gov/pdffiles1/digitization/149252ncjrs.pdf.

[2] S.2014. Missing Children's Assistance Act. https://www.congress.gov/bill/98th-congress/senate-bill/2014

[3] "Child Molesters: A behavioral analysis." National Center for Missing and Exploited Children in cooperation with the FBI. page v. https://www.ncjrs.gov/pdffiles1/digitization/149252ncjrs.pdf.

5

THE MODERN U.S. ABOLITIONISTS

Amy O'Neill Richard (Senior Advisor to the Director, Office to Monitor and Combat Trafficking in Persons [J/TIP])

> ## "ALL I COULD THINK TO DO WAS KEEP GOING. I WANTED TO BE PART OF THE SOLUTION AND KNEW THAT PEOPLE WOULD CARE IF THEY KNEW MORE. I SAID YES."
>
> ### AMY O'NEILL RICHARD

Shared Hope International was only a year old when the *New York Times* ran an article about child sex trafficking in the United States. Soon after, in 2000, an essential bill called the Trafficking Victims Protection Act (TVPA) was passed in Congress and signed by President Bill Clinton.

I would learn about one determined woman who was making an impact through her exhaustive research and her insatiable need to tell others the truth of her findings. Her research helped make the TVPA happen. Her efforts and dedication have often been somewhat

EARLIER THAN THE 1990S

Before the year 2000, the issue of sex trafficking was primarily unknown in America. Women and even underage girls and boys in prostitution were rarely considered to be victims. Child sex trafficking was generally thought to be a heinous problem, but in other countries far from the United States.

unknown, but her impact great. Amy O'Neill Richard is a powerhouse, and her story is one of a singular person following a childhood passion and pressing forward against obstacles or collaborating with a team to make an impact.

Amy holds an important place in bringing child sex trafficking and commercial sexual exploitation to the public arena. Without her, we may be much further behind than we are today. Here's Amy …

***

The first time I heard the words "trafficking" paired with "women," I was reading an article titled *Women's Vital Voices: The Costs of Exclusion in Eastern Europe* in the July/August 1997 edition of *Foreign Affairs* magazine and written by U.S. Ambassador to Austria Swanee Hunt.

It was the summer of 1997, and the article grabbed my attention. This was a transnational crime affecting vulnerable women

Among her many accomplishments, Ambassador Hunt went on to found Demand Abolition to eradicate the illegal commercial sex industry in the U.S.

and children in the newly independent states. I was working as an analyst for the State Department's Office of Terrorism, Narcotics, and Crime in the Bureau of Intelligence in Research.

My attention was further

captured when I read that trafficking of women was increasing exponentially. It was only six years after the breakup of the Soviet Union, so there was an East/West nexus, and the sex trade was fueling organized crime since traffickers capitalized on an expanding market, enormous profits, and minimal punishment.

When I was a young girl, I'd told my mother that I wanted to work on international human rights issues, especially in areas that impacted women and children. And as I read that article and thought about these women being forced into the sex trade for the profit of traffickers, the cogs in my brain started working:

I'm a transnational crime analyst stumbling upon this major transnational crime and human rights issue. I can do something.

I immediately wanted to apply my knowledge of organized crime and raise awareness. More people in government, and everywhere for that matter, needed to know about human trafficking.

It seemed so clear to me. If our government were combating drug smuggling and arms trafficking, of course they'd want to help stop the trafficking of women and children. What was more egregious than this? In America, the notion of a person being bought and sold as a commodity was so completely abhorrent, I firmly believed that action would follow knowledge.

Armed with my new knowledge from Ambassador Hunt's article, I went to my boss and explained that I wanted to do more research on the subject and to write about it.

"Isn't that a soft human rights issue?" he asked.

I was surprised by his reaction. We were focused on organized crime across nations. How could he not understand that this fit exactly within the purview of our work?

"Well, I beg to differ, but give me a few weeks to research it," I said, and then explained how sex trafficking was a political and economic issue that impacts relations between the origin and destination countries. It was certainly a transnational crime and corruption issue. With the crossing of borders, it was a migration issue. It was also a health issue. And no one could deny it was a human rights issue.

My boss was going out of town. It was summer, and so he gave me the go-ahead. I dove into whatever research I could find and set to work. A few months later, I'd written my first piece on the subject. It was an analyst's viewpoint: *International Trafficking of Women in Central Europe and the Newly Independent States.* Soon after I was asked to present the information from my paper at a U.S. and European Union forum in Luxembourg, and about this same time, I discovered a fellowship that would give me the chance to fully explore the issue internationally.

I went to my boss again and explained how I wanted to apply for the fellowship and focus more deeply on researching the trafficking industry around the world.

"I'm sorry, but this really isn't a good time," he began, and went on to give all the reasons why, how it would be tough to have a key staffer out, and that he needed me there.

I listened and thought it over for a while, then replied, "I understand, and I will stand down. But if in a year, I still want to do this and can find someone to replace me while I'm gone, can I apply for the fellowship then?"

He agreed. Over the months of the next year, my interest did not wane — they grew.

Not only did I believe it was essential to have a comprehensive report on the subject, but I also felt that if we at the State Department were encouraging other countries to combat trafficking, we had to understand the problem more fully inside the United States. This would make us more credible if we were open with our domestic shortcomings and demonstrated our willingness to collaborate with civil society and foreign governments on this major problem. I also wanted to learn exactly what was happening in the United States — we needed to clearly identify the traffickers, the facilitators, and those who were being trafficked.

A year later I found someone to cover my job, and my boss kept his end of the bargain. Then, I was selected for the fellowship. This began a year, from mid-1998 to mid-1999, when I researched and conducted

TRAFFICKING DEFINED

Trafficking in persons as defined by the United Nations is "the recruitment, transportation, transfer, harboring or receipt of persons, by means of the threat or use of force or other forms of coercion, of abduction, of fraud, of deception, of the abuse of power or of a position of vulnerability or of the giving or receiving of payments or benefits to achieve the consent of a person having control over another person, for the purpose of exploitation. Exploitation shall include, at a minimum, the exploitation of the prostitution of others or other forms of sexual exploitation, forced labour or services, slavery or practices similar to slavery, servitude or the removal of organs … The consent of a victim of trafficking in persons to the intended exploitation set forth [above] shall be irrelevant where any of the means set forth [above] have been used."[1]

interviews while I traveled nationally and internationally. I spent time at Interpol, interviewed defendants and anti-trafficking experts in countries around the world, studied every paper and statistic on the subject, and worked on compiling my report.

At times my research barreled over me like a tidal wave. In Asia, I went to red light districts and brothels where I met women and girls forced into commercial sexual exploitation with no hope of escape. These were often young girls, and always the pimps were nearby watching. The young women showed me their small rooms, essentially a table and mattress, with stuffed animals and pictures of Bollywood stars torn from magazines and tacked on the walls. I felt crestfallen, overwhelmed by the thought that these were children with the same hopes and dreams and Bollywood/Hollywood crushes of any girl of that age.

My heart broke. I felt powerless, especially with those pimps lurking in the shadows. I did not want to leave them behind. I felt my role was to share what I had seen and commit myself to do everything I could to fight for them. Still, for the individual girls who stared at me, it felt completely hollow.

Back home, I poured myself into the writing. One night, I sat on the floor of my row house with trafficking cases and papers circling me. Pausing a moment, I tried to catch my breath, but my heart felt heavy, like someone was pressing on it with a heavy weight. The images in my mind weren't only of women and girls in Asia, but also those from countries around the world. The papers held statistics and stories so tragic that I felt overwhelmed.

"It's just unconscionable," I muttered. I'd cried many times over the months of research, but now I bawled on the floor in my quiet home.

What was I doing? Would a single report make a difference? I asked myself, feeling helpless. But all I could think to do was keep going. I wanted to be part of the solution and knew that people would care if they knew more.

I'd been given office space through the President's Interagency Council on Women. In March of 1998 on International Women's Day, in the middle of my project, an executive memorandum was issued from the White House about combating trafficking of women and girls. The stars were aligning in a good way, and I knew my research would help.

In November 1999, I wrapped up my report: *International Trafficking in Women to the United States: A Contemporary Manifestation of Slavery and Organized Crime.*

I sat back looking at the pages and considered what to do next. This information was important, and I wanted policy-makers to read it. I didn't want it to become another report on an office shelf in D.C. I owed it to the victims that I met to make their stories known.

I went to Kinkos and bound copies myself to get it out faster. At an interagency meeting, I passed out the copies to each person there. Little did I know, and without my permission, somebody gave the report to the *New York Times.*

The story ran in the Times on April 2, 2000 (*C.I.A. Depicts a Vast Trade in Forced Labor*). I was stunned. Reuters, AP, and others picked up the story and my phone started ringing off the hook.

The timing was ripe. Already there were numerous civil society groups, faith-based groups, and NGOs lobbying for the passage of an anti-trafficking law.

TVPA OCTOBER 2000

The Trafficking Victims Protection Act of 2000 was introduced to the House by conservative Congressman Chris H. Smith (R-NJ).

Congressman Chris Smith has authored or coauthored nearly all of the trafficking bills and reauthorizations going through the House of Representatives each year.

The TVPA became a bipartisan law with Christian conservative Senator Sam Brownback (R-KS) and the late firebrand progressive Senator Paul Wellstone (D-MN) in the Senate. Wellstone and his wife were killed in a plane crash in 2002, after it was signed into law. The law was meant to combat trafficking in persons in the sex trade, slavery, and involuntary servitude.[2]

Its thirty-seven cosponsors were almost evenly spread between Democrats and Republicans. It was signed into law by President Bill Clinton.

Some of the politicians pushing the law pulled statistics and information from my report to use in their efforts to advocate for the law's passage.

In October 2000, the Trafficking Victims Protection Act passed. Now, at last, trafficking was defined, and there was a federal law with a victim-centered approach that prosecutors could use to prosecute traffickers and those who facilitate the crime.

The law called for the establishment of a new government office to lead U.S. global engagement and manage the coordination of federal efforts to combat human trafficking. The Trafficking in Persons office (TIP) was established in early 2001. As this new office was being put together, I received a call from the Under Secretary for Global Affairs Paula Dobriansky.

"I hear you've got some pretty good analytical research skills. Will you come head up the reports team?"

I had no doubt that this was

the right next step for me. I'd been so affected by the research, and this was exactly what I'd told my mother I wanted to do all those years ago. My mind went back to that day when I cried on my floor, feeling so helpless as the images and stories of the women and children I met surrounded me. I knew this was my chance to make a difference. I said yes. I felt very fortunate to be part of this small but mighty team, working to help build a new office to combat trafficking in persons. It was the opportunity to work with smart, talented people both inside and outside of the government, and to be part of a global movement to prevent women and children from being trafficked and to help protect future women and children from such exploitation and violence.

Two months after the TVPA passed, in December 2000, the United Nations held a high-level political conference in Palermo, Italy, to convene member states to sign a new

DECEMBER 2000

The United Nations Convention against Transnational Organized Crime is supplemented by a set of three protocols:

1. **Protocol to Prevent, Suppress and Punish Trafficking in Persons, especially Women and Children (also frequently referred to as the Palermo Protocol, Trafficking Protocol, UN TIP Protocol)**

2. **Protocol against the Smuggling of Migrants by Land, Sea and Air**

3. **Protocol against the Illicit Manufacturing of and Trafficking in Firearms**

According to the United Nations, "The (Palermo) Convention represents a major step forward in the fight against transnational organized crime and signifies

the recognition by Member States of the seriousness of the problems posed by it, as well as the need to foster and enhance close international cooperation in order to tackle those problems.

States that ratify this instrument commit themselves to taking a series of measures against transnational organized crime, including the creation of domestic criminal offenses (participation in an organized criminal group, money laundering, corruption and obstruction of justice); the adoption of new and sweeping frameworks for extradition, mutual legal assistance and law enforcement cooperation; and the promotion of training and technical assistance for building or upgrading the necessary capacity of national authorities."[3]

convention against Transnational Organized Crime. This was a multilateral convention supplemented by an international protocol against trafficking of persons, especially women and children.

These changes provided the tools to make an impact and a framework to strengthen prevention of the crime, protection for the victims, and prosecution of the traffickers. I moved to the new Department of State's Office to Monitor and Combat Trafficking in Persons, the TIP office. We didn't have working computers, FAX machines, or all of our furniture. When we were told that then-Deputy Secretary Richard Armitage was coming to do a ribbon-cutting, our office of six people felt like, "Wait, we don't have working equipment yet!" We were that small and that new, but the TIP office was operational. It was an exciting time.

My initial position was Senior Coordinator for the annual Trafficking in Persons (TIP) Report.

Because it was a new office, we were setting the policies, and designing and developing the new TIP Report that would become our signature report. My colleague Carla was developing our first international programs. It was a critical time, and I was tremendously grateful to be part of its creation.

The intellectual challenge was knowing that these policies would be analyzed for years to come, but there wasn't a playbook for us to work from. We didn't want to fail the anti-trafficking community, especially the trafficking survivors. Though we were a government office and carrying out foreign policy, we kept the victims at the forefront of our minds, which was a unique driver for all of us. We knew that we could be their voice — we didn't want to let them down.

The office needed an

2001 RELEASE OF FIRST TIP REPORT

"The Trafficking in Persons (TIP) Report is the U.S. Government's principal diplomatic tool to engage foreign governments on human trafficking. It is also the world's most comprehensive resource of governmental anti-human trafficking efforts and reflects the U.S. Government's commitment to global leadership on this key human rights and law enforcement issue. It represents an updated, global look at the nature and scope of trafficking in persons and the broad range of government actions to confront and eliminate it."[4] —U.S. Department of State website

ambassador at the helm. This stature was necessary for ensuring that the issue and office were taken seriously and was essential for our representation in high-level meetings at home and abroad. My first boss was Nancy Ely-Raphel, who was key as we were getting started that first year developing policies, programs, and the annual Trafficking in Persons Report. Next, former Congressman John R.

Miller was tapped to head up the office; his tenure ran from 2002–2006.

One central priority for Ambassador Miller was combating demand — predominately men who were seeking women and children to buy for sex. He wasn't afraid to color outside the lines if needed.

He'd call senior staff into his office and pitch an idea and then say, "That's my idea. Now tell me where I'm wrong, or talk me out of it."

But the issue was so important, and we were such a small office at the time, Ambassador Miller's ability to be hard-charging and mission-driven was necessary and helped us get a lot done.

Ambassador Miller was also caring. One Sunday when I was a new mom, he took the metro to my house so we could go over TIP Report narratives at my kitchen table. He didn't want me to have to travel and leave the baby to go into the office, even though work needed to get done.

Eventually, I moved from being Senior Coordinator to a Senior Advisor, which is more family-friendly since the TIP Report can be all-consuming. It also seemed the natural best step for me — as the issues calling to me were child trafficking, commercial sexual exploitation of children, and sex tourism of children, and being an advisor gave me the ability to focus on those areas exclusively.

Here I began work with incredible NGOs like Shared Hope International, ECPAT, World Vision, the Protection Project, as well as experts within the travel tourism and hospitality sector, and so many other dedicated U.S. government agency officers.

What I've discovered is that people who care about these

issues typically form a unique bond. The fight against human trafficking gets in your blood. Many natural synergies and friendships form because so many devoted, determined, and passionate people are banding together with a common purpose of eradicating modern slavery. That was exhilarating!

2000, 2003, 2005, 2008, 2013

Reauthorizations of the TVPA (Trafficking Victims Protection Act of 2000) have occurred to further strengthen the law or target areas of need in combating human trafficking.

Our office had a lot of work going on beyond the annual TIP Report. In April of 2003, the TVPA was reauthorized for the first time. With each reauthorization, our office was given additional mandates to implement.

The PROTECT (Prosecutorial Remedies and Other Tools to end the Exploitation of Children Today) Act was signed into law by President Bush in April 2003 and amended in May 2003 to enhance the ability of U.S. law enforcement to investigate and prosecute U.S. citizens and legal permanent residents who commit illicit sex acts against children abroad. The PROTECT Act had an important section devoted to countering the commercial sexual exploitation of children in travel and tourism.

At the time, I was responsible for furthering several initiatives to counter such exploitation, including a public awareness campaign against child sex tourism with World Vision. Our office also funded the Protection Project to do a major study on international child sex tourism and Shared Hope International's research on demand. We were engaging the travel, tourism,

SWEDEN 1996, JAPAN 2001, BRAZIL 2008

The First World Congress against Commercial Sexual Exploitation of Children was held in Stockholm, Sweden, in 1996. Queen Silvia of Sweden hosted the event co-sponsored by the NGO ECPAT that brought together an international gathering of law enforcement officials, NGOs (non-governmental organizations), corporations in the travel industry, and other groups. Queen Silva was given a TIP Report Hero Award in 2005 recognizing her contributions and her foundation's incredible work in combating trafficking around the world.

The Second World Congress was held in Yokohama, Japan, in 2001. At this gathering, countries had the opportunity to sign the Yokohama Global Commitment stating the commitments of nations to combat trafficking in their nations.

and hospitality sector, promoting signatories to the Code of Conduct for the Protection of Children from Sexual Exploitation in Travel and Tourism, working with ECPAT to counter child sex tourism, and putting on numerous awareness events — one was held at the United Nations with entertainer Ricky Martin, one at the World Bank with the Interfaith Center on Corporate Responsibility, and others at movie theaters or other venues, but always accompanied by expert discussions and informational resources. To enhance international engagement, there were the World Congresses against Commercial Sexual Exploitation of Children and our own World Summit.

Before the forming of the TIP office, the first World Congress was held in Stockholm, Sweden, in 1996. The second was in Yokohama, Japan, in 2001. The third was in Rio De Janeiro, Brazil, in 2008. These gatherings brought international experts from government, NGOs, and corporations where commitments were made to combat sexual exploitation of children and adolescents around the world, in the specific countries, and within industries.

I knew there was very good work going on in the United States in all of these areas. There was more to do, but I was proud of our progress. In between the World Congresses, countries and regions were to hold mid-term reviews to take stock of achievements obtained and remaining areas for improvement. Each agency was so focused on their work that it was challenging to devote time to arranging a symposium and all its associated logistics. I knew that if "we build it [the forum], they [the experts] would come." We just needed to figure out the venue and the logistics.

I remember going to coffee with Linda Smith, who is a wonderful gale of wind. When she comes in, she's going to do something — she is action-oriented, accomplishment-driven, and never says no.

So, I brought up the concept of a mid-term review and the need for a venue and organizer. "We can do this," Linda said, as I'd learn she'd often say. Shared Hope, the Protection Project, and ECPAT-USA went on to hold the event, and I set to organizing the U.S. government side. As predicted, every USG agency showed up and the officers went to work on analyzing where

2001 WATA (WAR AGAINST TRAFFICKING ALLIANCE) FORMED

Linda Smith initiated WATA, a coordinated regional and international effort to fight sex trafficking on a global scale. Alliance leaders included: The International Justice Mission, the Salvation Army, Johns Hopkins School of International Studies' Protection Project, and the United States Department of State.

we were achieving results and what areas we could improve upon.
Two years later following this mid-term review, I organized the U.S.
delegation, led by the Department of Justice, to World Congress III
against the Sexual Exploitation of Children and Adolescents.

This collaboration was not new, as our office had worked
with Linda Smith and Shared Hope International, along with
groups in WATA, to convene the first World Summit "Path-breaking
Strategies in the Global Fight Against Sex Trafficking" many years
prior. The State Department brought a senior person to our office to
work on developing the summit for six months. Initially planned for
early 2002, September 11th, 2001 delayed the event by a year.

The summit convened in February 2003, bringing activists
from 114 countries together to discuss practical solutions to prevent
and address sex tourism and commercial sex trafficking. We had
delegates from around the world get involved. Everyone was there to
enhance collaboration and discuss solutions. To me, it was this heady
feeling seeing so many leaders, experts, and activists all focused on
one central question, "How are we going to solve this?" In my mind,
that summit succeeded because of the commitments to address the
problem individually and collectively.

Over the years, developing partnerships and getting to know
the right people within the various USG agencies, NGOs, survivor
groups, and private sector companies has made all the difference,
since such partnerships leverage more expertise and resources.
I'm convinced if you know the pivotal person(s) within the faith-
based organization, NGO, survivor circles, or major corporation
— someone who is determined to make a difference — you can
accomplish extraordinary things. It takes people knowing what they

can accomplish in their respective space and how each person and entity can play to their comparative advantage. We each had a key piece in all that would come together in proceeding years as our collaboration continued to grow.

Over the years, people have asked me why I do it. Why do I keep fighting for this issue?

Frequently, people will ask, "Oh, it's so disheartening and depressing — how do you continue to work on this issue?"

My answer is two-fold.

One, there's something tremendously inspirational and empowering when you think about passionate, dedicated, and committed people in both the public and private sectors, who all come to the table with their respective strengths and talents determined to effect change. If we are applying ourselves and working together, we are a force to be reckoned with.

And two, I want to be part of a solution. What could be greater than building a modern abolitionist movement?

A relative of mine, Lucretia Mott, was a suffragette and an abolitionist in the 1800s, and I often think of her tenacity in fighting slavery and promoting women's rights. I also think of modern-day trafficking survivors. If they can keep going, rebuild their lives, and fight against the abuses they've endured, how can I give up?

Over the years, this all-important battle to combat child sex trafficking and commercial sexual exploitation of children has continued, and we have expanded our efforts to combat both sex trafficking and labor trafficking of men, women, and children.

I grew up being taught to *live your faith*. I hope at the end of my life to know that I've done just that.

[1] "Human Trafficking." United Nations Office on Drugs and Crime. https://www.unodc.org/unodc/en/human-trafficking/what-is-human-trafficking.html.

[2] Victims of Trafficking and Violence Protection Act of 2000. U.S. Department of State, https://www.state.gov/j/tip/laws/61124.htm.

[3] "United Nations Convention Against Transnational Organized Crime and Protocols Thereto." UNODC, https://www.unodc.org/unodc/treaties/CTOC/.

[4] "2018 Trafficking in Persons Report." U.S. Department of State, https://www.state.gov/j/tip/rls/tiprpt/.

6

ATLANTA'S CHILD IN SHACKLES

Deborah Richardson

"THESE ARE TRAFFICKED CHILDREN, NOT PROSTITUTES."

DEBORAH RICHARDSON

In the early 2000s, I heard about a group of women in Atlanta, Georgia, who were salvaging young lives and making incredible changes in their city.

The Trafficking Victim Protection Act (TVPA) was finally passed in 2000, and Shared Hope came alongside the Protection Project at Johns Hopkins University's School of Advanced International Studies to leverage that gain for the anti-trafficking movement. I traveled around the country explaining the TVPA to law enforcement and citizen groups at the state and local levels to help them implement the law into their practices. I was also doing research and meeting with other activists. In my travels, I heard about these women in Atlanta and decided to go meet them in person.

Before 2000, there was no law that directly punished traffickers of women and children. Traffickers enjoyed an endless market of women and children and had huge profits with low risks.

If traffickers, pimps, facilitators, and/or buyers (johns) were caught, punishment was usually minimal, if prosecuted at all.

Those who were arrested were most often the victims, even if under-aged, and charged with prostitution. If minors, their records might be sealed, but their criminal label and experiences remained with them.

At that time, most people thought trafficking in the United States meant the trafficked victims were brought from outside the U.S. — foreign victims — and were being forced into prostitution in the U.S. Few groups or agencies were focused on American children being bought and sold for sex. Few people would have believed it, and even I, myself, was just beginning to learn. This trip to Atlanta shocked me into understanding key pieces I'd been missing.

I don't remember what I was expecting, but when I arrived in Atlanta, this group of women blew me away as I saw them tackling pieces of the issue I hadn't fully grasped myself. It began with three women: Judge Nina R. Hickson, Commissioner Nancy Boxill, and Deborah Richardson. Their efforts grew to include other dynamic women including Stephanie Davis, Mayor of Atlanta Shirley Franklin, Shelley Senterfitt (who was the first lobbyist), Alicia Adams (the first employee), Kayrita M. Anderson, Katie McCullough, Sherri Fallin-Simmons, Sharon Saffold, Beth Schapiro, Janice Barrocas, and State Senator Renee S. Unterman.

It's interesting that the way things have always been done can really blind us to what *should* be done — can blind us to how something terribly wrong can become institutionalized in our society. Standard procedure dictated that people caught in prostitution were arrested. And as a matter of routine, kids were being arrested, charged, and convicted for prostitution according to that same unquestioned standard procedure.

Deborah Richardson said words I'll never forget: "These are trafficked children, not prostitutes."

She was right. A kid shouldn't be labeled as a prostitute, and under the TVPA, they were human-trafficking victims.

I'd been working with girls who were domestically trafficked in India. That meant that men were buying sex acts with girls in their own country, because they considered these girls to be lesser human beings. But the same injustice was happening in our country too — American men were buying sex acts with American kids.

It was an *aha* moment for me. *Of course, a child is a victim and is not choosing to go into prostitution. So why are they arrested as prostitutes? Why is this happening?*

Then Deborah told me about her own moment of revelation and what happened afterward that sparked so much change in Atlanta. She told me a story I wouldn't forget.

In 1999, Juvenile Court Judge Nina Hickson had been shocked to see the growing number of young defendants in her court being brought before her as "prostitutes." This was just three years after Atlanta had modernized and upgraded to host the summer Olympics, yet she had no laws or means to help these kids. There were dozens of young women coming into her court in shackles. The average age was 14. Some were as young as 10. They were white, black, city kids, suburban, and rural and all brought to Atlanta by pimps to meet the multi-million-dollar demand.

It was later discovered that advertising in places like New York invited johns to not travel all the way to Bangkok when they could go to Atlanta instead.

Judge Hickson knew she needed help if anything were to change. As a judge, she had to make her decisions based on law and the best means to protect these young women. There were no good solutions. She met with Deborah, who was the Director of Program Development for Fulton County Juvenile Court. Then Deborah saw the problem for herself.

One morning as she was sitting in the back of the courtroom, the clack of shackles and feet shuffling across the floor caught Deborah's attention. As Director of Program Development for Fulton County Juvenile Court, her job was to help families and kids connect to social services early in the court process, and she had developed new programs to help those struggling families. When she looked up at that sound, she saw a young girl shuffling to the front of the courtroom. The girl's hands were in cuffs in front of her, her feet in shackles. Her hair was messy, eyes cast downward. She sat down and seemed to make herself as small as possible.

Something about the girl caught Deborah's attention in a different way. It wasn't only that she appeared incredibly young. Deborah knew that most children frantically looked around for their parents in the courtroom, but this girl seemed to have no one. She sat compliant and emotionless, staring at the floor. What could this child have done?

Deborah leaned forward as the proceeding began, eager to

hear what the girl was being charged with. As the charges were read, she felt numb. She shook her head, leaning in further to make sure she was hearing correctly. Curfew violation? This young girl was arrested, handcuffed and shackled, and brought before a judge for being out after the city's 11:00 p.m. curfew?

It didn't make sense.

Then Deborah heard the situation surrounding her broken curfew charge and felt a sickened rage rise within the pit of her stomach. In a public park, the child was found in the back seat of a van with a 42-year-old man. He had rented the girl for two hours of sex.

How could this child be arrested when a heinous crime was being committed *against her*? Deborah couldn't believe what she was hearing. She soon found out that the man who paid to have sex with the girl had received a misdemeanor and a $50 fine — the equivalent of a traffic ticket. In the state of Georgia, pimping and pandering a minor was only a misdemeanor. The man was free to go, while this girl was brought in shackles before a judge.

When Deborah met with Judge Hickson, she was even more horrified by what she heard.

"I see twenty to thirty kids just like that girl being brought through my courtroom every week," Judge Hickson said.

The problem was the law. But this wasn't justice. How could it be happening, and why wasn't anyone stopping it? Deborah couldn't believe that children were being exploited in such a monstrous manner. She made a commitment to herself that it was going to stop.

Deborah and Judge Hickson brought in Commissioner

Nancy Boxill. Fueled by their outrage, they helped mobilize the women of their community. Mothers, daughters, and sisters all united for a common cause: fighting the trafficking and sexual exploitation of children. Together they came up with a three-pronged strategy:

On January 7, 2001, The *Atlanta Journal-Constitution* published a special report: *Selling Atlanta's Children.*

The report helped awaken the people of Atlanta to the problem of child sex trafficking and included the story of a defendant dressed in standard jail clothing — "navy jumpsuit, orange T-shirt, orange socks and orange plastic flip-flops. Metal shackles around her ankles..."

The defendant was a 10-year-old girl, a runaway, and an alleged prostitute. Her 11-year-old sister had been arrested with her.

This special report and others like it helped to deploy the community into action to stop the trafficking of minors in Atlanta and to create places to help these victimized kids.

1. Educate the community about what was happening in their city — that kids were being sold for sex on their streets. They enlisted the help of the Atlanta newspapers and media outlets.

2. Find or establish a place for these young women to get help. Often judges like Judge Hickson kept the kids in jail or juvenile detention because there were no other options to keep them safe and off the streets. While this kept them safe, it created many other problems for the girls. It made them criminals.

3. Advocate for legislative changes, including making it a felony to pimp and pander a child.

Their determination and resilience paid off. In less than two years, these women made enormous progress. They advocated for a new law making it a felony to pay to have sex with a child. They'd started in September, and, by January, Senate Bill 33 passed both houses of Georgia's state legislature. It was signed into law by Governor Roy Barnes in March 2001.

The women also raised $1 million and opened a shelter for minors who were victims of trafficking. By February 2002, Angela's House began to accept referred kids.

However, changing minds proved even harder than changing laws. Deborah discovered how deeply entrenched the perceptions of law enforcement and social agencies were toward these kids. They viewed them as being part of the crime even though the crime was being committed against them. It was a long-held view attached to the word "prostitution." It created a belief that these kids were culpable instead of victimized.

Deborah heard a popular state Senator stand up at a committee meeting and say, "You cannot stop prostitution. It's the oldest profession in the world."

She responded, "We aren't talking about prostitution. We are talking about young girls being bought and sold."

This courageous group of women from Atlanta kept pressing and gradually began seeing real change, chipping away at the laws. Public meetings were helpful, newspapers reported on the problem, and awareness grew. Five years later, it became mandatory for hotels and places of service to post a sign stating that trafficking was outlawed. The sign included a toll-free hotline. This became a warning to pimps and buyers of children that they'd be charged with a felony now. The toll-free number gave trafficked victims and people who suspected trafficking a free way to get help.

They also saw mindsets change. Trainings with law enforcement and government groups depicted these kids as victims, not criminals. Safe Harbor laws referred children for services instead of criminal records.

Deborah Richardson has a 30-year track record in program development, administration, and fundraising. As an advocate on child sexual exploitation, Deborah has designed leading programs for girls victimized by commercial sexual exploitation and has led the Women's Funding Network's national initiative, *A Future. Not A Past.*, focused on working with women's funds and community organizations across the U.S. to prevent and end domestic minor sex trafficking. She was Executive Vice President of the National Center for Civil and Human Rights in Atlanta, then founded the International Human Trafficking Institute as an initiative of the Center. She is currently leading a

There were more battles ahead. Many more. But the changes were incredible.

As I heard Deborah's and the other women's stories, I was fueled by the same anger and resolve to do something. "You have been part of my education," I told Deborah.

I thought of those kids being charged with crimes related to their trafficking, and how from then on, they'd have a record for prostitution, or curfew violation, or shoplifting, or carrying drugs for the pimp. And the *kids* were put into shackles. To some degree I could understand the motivation to treat them this way. It was the idea that an arrest would get them off the streets and away from pimps and the dangers associated with prostitution like physical abuse, torture, and murder. The reasoning was that shackles and tough treatment, including juvenile hall, might just wake these young women up. But that mentality was wrong.

These young women didn't need a wake-up call. They hadn't chosen this path. If they were runaways, they had run from a bad situation in the first place. These kids couldn't stay in detention forever, and when they were released, they went right back to the pimps. They didn't have another place to go besides the same situation — except now they had a record. Now the girls were criminals.

three-year community-wide public and private effort to address human trafficking in Metro Atlanta focusing on reducing the demand for persons sold for sexual or labor purposes.

She is the co-author of *Ending Sex Trafficking of Children in Atlanta* (Affilia: "Journal of Women and Social Work," Spring 2007). (Huffpost)

This mentality was pervasive across America. The rest of the country was treating them like criminals as well. It wasn't just Atlanta.

But here was a group of women in Georgia — the very first group I saw that was pulling children from the juvenile justice system and treating them as victims instead of as criminals. These women were fighting to get the kids off the streets, give them some hope and safety, change the laws to help them, and get justice for their victimizers. This small group of individuals with a singular cause had gotten a law changed and raised over a million dollars in such a short amount of time.

The culture, "the way it has always been," was against them. They made the changes anyway.

Georgia became one of the first in the country to change state laws to protect trafficked victims. They've put notorious pimps in prison with 30-year prison sentences. They've secured funding from the Georgia legislature for a regional assessment center to provide a safe haven for young women victimized in sex trafficking. And it all happened because of these trail-blazing women.

I left Atlanta ready to carry a torch like theirs. The entire country needed this kind of change, and it needed people to make it happen.

7

A Victim's Story

THEY CHOOSE THOSE ALREADY IN PAIN.

Belle felt the cold vinyl of the police car against her as she tried to shrink back against the seat as if she might disappear from the officer's view. Her wrists ached from the handcuffs, and they cut into her skin when she moved to the edge of the seat and tried to push down her short pink skirt. She tried remembering what Jerome had told her to do if the police picked her up. He'd said, "Don't you forget any of this, or you'll be in worse trouble." But Belle only remembered him saying to never get arrested.

"You'll be a ho and a criminal like half of the girls there," he'd said.

Belle closed her eyes, wishing she could go back in time. Back to when she was little again. Back when she'd climb into bed with her mom when she woke up scared during the night. She loved her mother's perfume and how warm it felt in her bed under the thick quilt her grandma had hand-sewn. Grandma had promised to teach Belle to sew someday, but someday had never come.

Belle tried shaking away the old memories before her eyes welled up with tears. She could not let herself cry. What good would it do except make somebody angry? She'd learned that tears brought anger, and sometimes more pain. It was better to forget that she'd ever had a home. She couldn't call her mom, and Grandma was gone now.

"If you call or go back, I'll hurt all of them," Jerome had warned. The other girls repeated his warning, especially in the beginning when she'd cried all the time. Tink had told her that tears brought Jerome's wrath and to believe his threats.

"He'll hurt you, and he'll hurt anyone who goes against him," Tink had told her. "And your family don't want you now anyway. Nobody wants their whore daughter back in the house. You're soiled goods now, girl. You belong where we're all the same and there's no judgment. We accept you just how you are."

Belle had once believed that Jerome loved her. He'd been such a good boyfriend for a long time. But then he got himself into trouble. He owed someone money and needed her to help him out. She could remove his debt if she did one thing for him. That one thing was a man. He gave her some pills to make it easier, and afterward, he moved her to Kansas City, the biggest city she'd been to. But moving her to the city was the only promise he fulfilled. Once there, she met the other girls and became one of them, not Jerome's one and only.

They were all named after Disney characters. Belle's real name was Jill. That sounded strange on her lips now. At night, she sometimes curled up and said it in her mind. My name is Jill. My name is Jill. What if one day she lost herself completely and forgot who she was? There had to be more than this life. She knew there was, because she used to have it. But it was fading with every month, and she wondered if by the time she turned 15 it might be completely gone.

Outside the police car, Belle watched the man nodding his head as he talked to the police officer. The man looked her way for a moment and his face was lit briefly by the flashing blue and red lights. Belle had overheard Jerome say that she cost $150 and $500 for the whole night. Usually Belle's "dates" were in the backseat of a john's car or maybe a smelly rundown motel. This was the first time she'd come to a house in the nice part of town. The house looked like a mansion to Belle with the fountain out front and a swimming pool in back. She'd never been in a place this nice, or at such a fancy party. Jerome had given her a pink dress and new high-heeled shoes still in the box. Tink told her she was lucky to get this, that the client liked younger girls, under 15, with large dark eyes and long hair.

Belle found it funny that Tink used the word "the client" instead of "john." But she didn't find it funny when she met him. He was older than her stepdad and twice his size. He welcomed her into the house where a party was going on. They walked through the rooms and Belle wondered if she would ever be able to find her way back to the front door.

"Maybe you can take a swim later," he said, looking down at her.

The pool did look nice, but Belle felt nervous around the man. She tried to remember everything she'd been told.

She passed through the living room and saw other young women, some sitting on the laps of men, others dancing in front of the window. It smelled like cigarettes, alcohol, and flowers. The large man led her into a side room and closed the door, ordering her to remove her clothes. He was sweaty and looking at his cell phone. She'd been there an hour when the cops busted in. Then the entire house turned to chaos.

Belle found her clothes and wished she could use the bathroom. She didn't know where the man had disappeared to. She thought of running but knew she would never find the exit in that place. A cop asked her age and she said 18 instead of 14. But people always said she looked young, maybe younger than 14, and Belle knew the cop didn't believe her.

She was led to the door with her wrists handcuffed. As they moved through the house, Belle saw other people handcuffed like she was. One of the dancing girls was sobbing in a corner.

Down the cobblestone walk, the heel of her shoe caught between the stones and broke as she stumbled. The policeman paused just a moment, then pressed her to hurry up toward the cop car as she limped on the one broken heel.

She sat in the back of that car, looking at the beautiful house. Now she'd have a record too. Everything was just like Jerome had said. She'd never call home now. Who would want a convict for a kid? As soon as she could, Belle would go back to Jerome and the girls. There was no other place for her now.

***

Belle is fictionalized from true stories, and I've heard scenarios like Belle's countless times. Young women lured into trafficking after being targeted in their community, or runaways out on the street trying to survive. Today, much of the facilitation is done online. But still the connection of luring young women into trafficking continues.

Some ways in which pimps break down a girl's will:

1. This girl was lured into trafficking. Only on rare occasions are girls kidnapped — the majority are coerced and lured.

2. Victimization becomes twisted for these kids. Though she has few choices in her situation, she believes that she is culpable in her victimization. She is doing criminal acts. Though she is forced to do them, this concept is twisted into her believing that she is doing wrong instead of wrong being done to her.

3. Even she believes she is a whore and a criminal.

4. Instead of seeing law enforcement as her rescuer, she's been convinced that the police are there to inflict further harm — make her a criminal.

5. Many survivors of child sex trafficking cannot get employment because they have criminal records based on their abuse and exploitation. This is another form of abuse and another piece that hinders them from rebuilding their lives.

8

TRAFFICKING DYNAMICS

Samantha Healy Vardaman

"IT WAS MODERN SLAVERY."
SAMANTHA HEALY VARDAMAN

I first met Samantha Vardaman on the other side of the globe in a country I had to search for on a map. The Republic of Moldova was a newly established nation that had broken off from the Soviet Union less than a decade and a half earlier. It was challenged with the transition from communism to a democratic government, its economy had tanked, and it had a major problem: its young people were disappearing.

Samantha was a young American attorney working in Moldova with the American Bar Association's Central European and Eurasian Law Initiative (CEELI) to help build the country's legal system. When we briefly met while working on a major event in the country's capital, I couldn't have guessed what an invaluable asset

Samantha would become to not only Shared Hope International, but to the fight against sex trafficking around the world and in the United States. But before I share more about those stories, I'll let Samantha tell about her journey into fighting domestic minor sex trafficking …

***

I discovered human trafficking and the myriad effects it had on a nation's community, economy, and legal system by way of the Republic of Moldova. I wasn't in the country for the purpose of discovery; I'd come to use my law skills to join the effort to build the nation's legal system. Yet the issue kept coming around.

Right out of law school, I started practicing law with a firm in Washington, D.C. I soon felt the itch to do something different. I envisioned working in a Latin or South American country where I could put my years of high school and college Spanish to good use. But a close friend and fellow attorney brought up Moldova.

"Where?" I asked. My friend told me it would be great.

I had followed the work of the American Bar Association Central European and Eurasian Law Initiative (ABA/CEELI) that helped the New Independent States of the former Soviet Union transition and grow the rule of law. The ABA relied on volunteer attorneys providing pro bono work in these nations for three weeks to one year. While in the country, attorneys would offer their expertise in addressing the most pressing problems that each particular country faced. ABA/CEELI was running a successful program growing pro bono legal services through the establishment of law school clinics that appealed to me.

The Republic of Moldova is a small Eastern European country about the size of Maryland. The predominant language is Romanian, though many Moldovans speak Russian, Ukrainian, and a Turkic language called Gagauz. My Spanish wouldn't be helpful there. The American Bar Association's Central European Law Initiative was created after the fall of the Soviet Union in 1990 with the goal of building up the judicial systems of newly established democratic countries. It was funded through the U.S. government as a commitment to improve former Soviet countries, get their legal systems up to democratic standards, and to help them not devolve back into communism.

In 2002, I arrived in the capital city of Chisinau. The program provided my room, board, and a small stipend. I didn't need much anyway. The country was still rebuilding even though a decade had passed since the fall of the Berlin Wall — the lead domino knocking out the communist hold on country after country in the former USSR. I could see the communist past around the city mixed with its more ancient history and the new struggling democracy. Stoic gray structures marked with graffiti and decay stood amidst old cathedrals. New construction rose from the rubble of dilapidated buildings, but often the workers used outdated practices, hand tools, and rickety scaffolding that would make many building contractors cringe.

When I went out at night, I soon learned from other expats to carry a flashlight and to watch out for open potholes in the streets. Light bulbs were regularly stolen from street lights for their filament, and manhole covers were taken and sold for their metal. The country was struggling, and the poverty was painful to see. At that time,

Moldova was the poorest country in Eastern Europe. It had the lowest average salary of former Soviet Union countries — around $30 a month in U.S. currency. This income was nearly impossible to live on, and women's salaries were 70 to 80 percent less than the men's. Eighty percent of the population in Moldova lived below the poverty line.

I soon loved the people and the country. I volunteered for one year, but when my term was finished, I applied for a contract position. I was hired as the ABA/CEELI Country Director for the Moldova office.

I'd become somewhat conversant in Romanian and now felt at home in the city. But as progress was made in the legal system, I discovered another problem — both stunning and awful — that was woven into a large majority of the cases I was seeing in the pro bono law clinics. Moldovans would walk into the clinic seeking legal advice with a frequently common underlying cause: human trafficking.

There were child custody cases, like a grandmother who needed legal guardianship over her grandchildren. The woman's daughter had left the country temporarily for a job in Portugal while her children remained with the grandmother. The daughter promised to send money and to keep in close contact. For the first few weeks after she left, the daughter called, but then there was nothing. The grandmother hadn't been able to reach her daughter after that. She'd had no word in two years. As worried as she was about her daughter, the grandmother needed legal guardianship of her grandchildren to enroll them in school and to make decisions for medical care. Houses were in foreclosure because the owner left for an "opportunity" out of Moldova and never returned. Divorces, death certificates, business ownership, and other cases were all connected to these stories.

Moldovans were being trafficked out of the country at an alarming rate. Soon, it was estimated that 25 percent of the young people in Moldova were victims of human trafficking, including forced labor, organ trafficking, and the sex trade. Later, the amount of internal, domestic human trafficking would increase as the economy grew.

A young person was offered work, and the job looked legitimate. Traffickers often went to great lengths, sometimes using authentic labor contracts to reassure prospective victims of the genuine job offer to make a proposal appear genuine; other times, people desperate for opportunity wanted to believe the fake offers were real. One project attempting to address trafficking recruitment funded a hotline that checked the status of the company and the job. But despite awareness and prevention efforts, soon the young person was moved out of Moldova and exploited in another country — all to feed a ravenous appetite for commercial sex. Moldovan men and children were often trafficked to Russia and other countries for forced labor or forced begging. Women and children were enslaved in brothels with threats toward their families back home if they resisted or tried to escape. This was the dynamic that faced the country and the region broadly.

What was happening in Moldova was what people typically expected trafficking to look like: illegal migration. The very term "trafficking" conjured up elements of movement and transportation. Later, this view of human trafficking was a hurdle in understanding its true scope. Trafficking isn't about migration or movement — it is instead an issue of people being exploited by others. It is modern slavery.

In Moldova, human-trafficking laws were passing slowly and with little resources to implement them to protect citizens or to prosecute these often sophisticated and wealthy predators. Human trafficking was big business, and the instability in the country allowed these predators to profit, making trafficking an appealing job option for many young men and sometimes women spotting the opportunity.

It was about this time that Shared Hope International was commissioned by the U.S. Department of State Trafficking in Persons Office to hold national summits in countries that were falling behind in combatting human trafficking. Moldova was at the top of the list. My team at ABA/CEELI was asked to provide on-the-ground leadership and coordination.

In 2003, 2004, and 2005, "Next Steps" conferences were held in global locations including: Moldova, India, Indonesia, South Africa, Dominican Republic, and Singapore.

Since Shared Hope didn't have an office in the country, they asked if ABA/CEELI could help prepare for the conference. In the months leading up to it, changes were being made. A law was passed to make trafficking illegal in the country, but that didn't mean traffickers would be arrested and prosecuted. Awareness was low, resources were tight, and traffickers didn't seem deterred by the new law at all.

The two-day event in May 2003 was titled *Pathbreaking Strategies in the Global Fight Against Sex Trafficking Conference.* The goal was to bring together the country's top governmental leadership and representatives from the EU, international nonprofit organizations, and nearly twenty embassies from around the world.

As I worked with Shared Hope International to organize the event, I became further aware of the problem ravaging this country as well as other nations. The U.S. Embassy in Moldova was a key contributor in the organization of the event. The outcome of the conference was a Next Steps document to press forward changes to address the identified problems. A new national human-trafficking coalition in Moldova led by the Organization for Security and Cooperation in Europe (OSCE) would implement the Next Steps.

In 2005, it was time to say good-bye to this country I'd grown to love. While looking for a position in the U.S., I heard about a need at the D.C. office of Shared Hope International.

I'd been impressed with their global efforts and had enjoyed my previous connections with the organization, and my skills and experiences were especially equipped for the position. I was brought on for a new project commissioned by the U.S. Department of State. The project involved researching and producing a report and awareness documentary on sex trafficking in four countries around the globe. This Demand Report was intended to examine sex tourism and sex trafficking in countries that varied in culture, size, economy, political system, and history of sex tourism and slavery. The chosen nations were the Netherlands, Jamaica, Japan, and the United States.

The Demand Report did

> **In 2005, the Demand research began examining the marketplace of sex trafficking — defined as the buying and selling of humans for the purposes of sexual exploitation in exchange for anything of value — in four countries: Jamaica, Japan, the Netherlands, and the United States.**

something more than just offer a comparison of nations and reveal their issues with sex trafficking … it exposed a huge problem right under our noses.

Sure, everyone knew that the issue existed in the United States, but suddenly we made a sharp turn as the research revealed just how vast and complex sex trafficking was right here in the U.S. — and not just with foreign victims brought illegally to the country. What stunned us all was the number of American kids listed as "missing" who'd ended up in the commercial sex-trafficking industry and the predominant number of men who were buying sex with kids.

I was reminded of my slow discovery in Moldova, but this was something else. I'd been fighting battles away from home only to discover there was a war destroying my own country, and I hadn't known anything about it. As an attorney, I was furious to discover just how much the laws and policies of our own nation were failing the very kids it was meant to protect. Buyers of children were rarely prosecuted in these cases. A child molested by his neighbor might get services and see the predator prosecuted, but children sold to sexual abuse again and again were treated as delinquents and sent to detention with a record that would plague them long after. The system was a disaster.

"We've got to change these laws," Linda said. "These are children, they can't be called *child prostitutes*. They are victims. We need to change the way people talk about them to help change the way the world views them."

I knew by now that this woman, who although small in stature, was a force to be reckoned with, and I knew we could make changes. We had to.

TRAFFICKING DYNAMICS

A new direction for Shared Hope was being formed. I didn't leave SHI after the Demand Report was completed — there was too much to do. In the fight against trafficking in the United States, I was just getting started.

The process of producing the Demand Report was complicated, but it yielded such substantial material on domestic trafficking of U.S. citizen/lawful permanent resident (LPR) children that the Department of Justice found it interesting and persuasive. Thus, the DOJ approved our application to work with 10 newly funded human-trafficking task forces across the country with the goal of developing knowledge and protocols to identify victims of what we termed "Domestic Minor Sex Trafficking" (DMST) and respond to them with access to services rather than arrest. This project became the cornerstone of research and training on DMST. Fourteen local assessments later, in 2009, SHI published the *National Report on Domestic Minor Sex Trafficking*.

At a hearing before the House Judiciary Subcommittee on Crime, Terrorism, Homeland Security and Investigations on

2007 — Demand Report and documentary are released.

September 15, 2010, Linda Smith testified on the issue, and this research was admitted into the Congressional Record as definitive and authoritative research on sex trafficking of U.S. citizens and lawful permanent resident children. It also firmly established the term Domestic Minor Sex Trafficking (DMST) and altered the landscape of identification, response, and prevention going forward.

9

A Victim's Story

In 1998, when I was starting Shared Hope International, I had no idea the extent of America's problem that remained hidden to me. While today, much of the luring of victims occurs over the Internet and on social media sites, for the longest time it was all done face-to-face. It was a complex and systematic approach that pimps took (and still take today, both online and off) to lure young women and girls into sex trafficking. There is an actual *Pimps Playbook* that teaches how to manipulate and prey on the most vulnerable in America — children. Often these predators use the tactics of love and attention on girls they've targeted who are rarely getting love or attention in their homes. They choose those already in pain.

Ashley is a fictionalized character based on real young women who were targeted and their lives forever altered by being lured and then forced into sexual slavery. I have met hundreds of American girls and their families with stories like this. None survive unscathed, if they survive at all …

***

Portland, OR, 1998

"I'd like to pay for that," a guy's voice said over Ashley's shoulder as she dug through her purse.

The girl behind the cash register of the smoothie shop tapped her fingernails on the counter beside the contents of Ashley's purse that were splayed out like a crime scene.

"I got it, somewhere in here," she muttered, as a few coins tumbled from her wallet onto the tile floor. She dove to grab them as the guy behind her laughed and stepped around her, taking out his wallet.

Ashley stared at his shoes for a second and then popped up with the coins. He had blonde hair swept across his forehead, tan skin, and a wide grin. His hazel eyes met hers, and she caught her breath.

"But I ordered three — for me and my friends. It was my turn to buy."

"No problem."

He slid out a twenty from among other crisp bills she saw. His arm accidentally brushed hers sending a shiver through her. Ashley felt herself turn red, but she focused on stuffing her purse with the Harry Potter Chamber of Secrets book she'd recently checked out, a pink hair scrunchy, and the makeup she'd bought at the Dollar Store.

"You're doing me a favor," the guy said as they moved over to wait for the order.

"How am I doing you a favor?" This made her laugh a little

and feel more comfortable, but the guy was just so much older, and cute!

"You're letting me be a chivalrous guy when people say that chivalry is dead."

Ashley wasn't exactly certain what *chivalrous* meant, except that she felt it was related to knights and damsels in distress.

"Well, then you're welcome," she said, grinning up at him as he laughed. She was tall for her age, taller than most of the boys in her freshman class, so she wasn't used to looking up to a guy.

"Where are you sitting?" he asked.

Ashley pointed to Jessica and Sarah over in the corner of the food court.

"Over there."

He picked up the tray of smoothies and smiled. Ashley stood frozen, staring, and unsure of what to do or say next.

"After you," he said, bowing slightly.

She shuffled ahead of him and walked toward her friends, trying to play it cool. Jessica and Sarah were gaping, kicking themselves under the table. He set the tray down and smiled at the girls.

"Hi. I'm Jason," he said more to Ashley than to her friends.

"Ashley. I'm Ashley."

"Well, Ashley, do you mind if I join you?"

"Uh, no. He paid for our smoothies," Ashley said to Jessica and Sarah who grinned as they said hello and gave their names.

The girls squirmed in their seats. Jason was polite but kept turning his attention to Ashley.

Jason was amazing. The girls couldn't believe he was sitting at their table. He was friendly to all of them, but Ashley felt like his smile was just for her. They talked about school and friends and some family stuff. Ashley's friends finally left them at the table to walk around the mall, and Ashley barely noticed them leave. Jason told her about taking a semester off from college to start his own business and how it was going so well that he wasn't planning to return to school in the fall. But mostly, he asked about her. When Sarah and Jessica returned, Ashley realized they'd been talking for more than an hour.

Before Jason left, he pulled out a Nokia cell phone and asked Ashley for her number.

She bit her lip.

"I don't have a cell phone, and my grandparents don't really like guys calling at their house."

Jason smiled as if this was perfectly fine. "Could you meet here again, next Saturday?"

Jessica and Sarah giggled as Ashley nodded. She couldn't believe someone in his twenties, who had his own business, would be interested in her. For the entire week, Ashley thought of Jason nearly every minute. She regretted not giving him her number, or at least getting his. What if he wasn't at the mall and she never saw him again?

The next Saturday afternoon Ashley's grandpa dropped her off, and Jason was sitting at the corner table in the food court. He already had a smoothie waiting for her; the same kind she'd ordered last week. He stood as she approached the table, then gave her a long hug.

"This might sound crazy, but I've missed you," he said softly in her ear.

Ashley felt a shiver of warmth right down to her toes. She sat down with her smoothie and took a sip.

"I haven't been able to stop thinking about you. How was your week?" he asked, scooting his chair close to her.

"It was okay. I'm kind of bored now that school is out. My grandparents don't really let me do anything fun," Ashley shrugged.

"So tell me about your grandparents."

Ashley took another sip of her smoothie. Jason was so easy to talk to. She told him all about her mom, how she had been in and out of rehab for years. No one knew where she was right now, and Ashley was worried about her. As she talked, emotion rose in her chest and she feared she might cry. Jason put a reassuring hand on hers. He made her feel so safe. She told him about her dad, that he lived in a trailer in the backyard of her grandparents' house. He rarely came in the house for dinner anymore. He was always out in the back or in the trailer with his friends. And he was always drunk. Ashley was afraid of his friends.

"I really love the outfit you have on today. And the way you do your makeup. It's really beautiful."

Ashley blushed and took another sip of her smoothie. She had copied the makeup looks from a book she had checked out at the city library. She had hoped he would notice.

"So what else are you doing this summer?" he asked.

"Nothing much. My grandma finally let me sign up for a dance class at the community center," she said, smiling.

"I knew it! You're a dancer!"

"Well, kind of. My mom took me a couple of times to ballet when I was little. I loved it. I practice by myself all the time and checked out a bunch of books about it. My friends say I'm a natural." She couldn't hold back her excitement when talking about dancing, and Jason seemed so intrigued.

"That's so cool. But what do you mean your grandma 'finally' let you sign up?"

"Oh, she just kept saying I should spend more time on other things like reading. She really wants me to get into a good college someday. I get good grades, it's just never good enough for her," Ashley said.

"Look, Ashley, I'm sure your grandparents love you. They are just too old to really understand what you're going through."

"My Grandma says I'm an old soul," Ashley shrugged.

"Well I can see what she's saying. I mean, you seem so much older. I think you're amazing. In fact, I bought you something. A present."

"A present?"

"Yes," he smiled. "I told you, I've missed you."

Jason pulled a small box out of his pocket. Ashley opened it. Inside was a pair of earrings.

"They're beautiful. They look like diamonds," she said.

"They are. I told you my business is going well, and you deserve so much more in life. You deserve someone who understands you. I work really hard, but I know what it's like to be lonely."

Ashley was speechless. Jason held back her hair and stroked her neck as she put the earrings in her ears. She shivered.

"Listen, I want to introduce you to my friends. Would that be OK?"

Ashley nodded, smiling. She still couldn't believe she was

wearing real diamonds.

"And here's the best part," Jason grabbed her hand and squeezed it. "My friend owns a dance studio."

"A dance studio?"

"Yes. And I'll bet if I ask him he would let you dance there. How would you like that?"

"I don't know. When?"

"How about tonight? Can you tell your grandparents you're staying over with one of your friends? Maybe you can just call them right now."

Ashley nodded. She hated lying to her grandparents, but there was no way they would let her hang out with Jason.

"But, do you think I'll really fit in with your friends?" she asked.

"Don't be silly. Why don't I take you shopping? We can find something for you to wear tonight. Would that make you feel more comfortable?"

Ashley was thrilled. She couldn't wait to meet Jason's friends and check out the dance studio. It seemed as if all of her dreams were coming true. She had a rich, handsome, older guy acting like he wanted to be her boyfriend and take care of her.

"What's the dance studio like? What's it called?"

"Oh," he said, "It's called the Sugar Shack. You're going to love it. Trust me. Everyone's going to love you, too."

10

SEEKING JUSTICE

Drew Oosterbaan

"IT'S HAVING A VISION AND DEVISING A WAY TO ACCOMPLISH IT — THAT'S WHAT GETS ME UP IN THE MORNING. THAT'S WHAT KEEPS ME GOING."
DREW OOSTERBAAN

As a new millennium began in 2000, only two short years after my first trip to Mumbai, I was immersed in creating services for trafficking survivors abroad, and Shared Hope International had just established the Women's Investment Network (WIN), empowering women in India (and eventually all over the world) to support themselves and their children. The following year we would form the War Against Trafficking Alliance to coordinate regional and international efforts to fight sex trafficking on a global scale. From where I sat, pieces were coming together as nations began collaborating to fight trafficking around the world.

This same year, the Trafficking Victims Protection Act of 2000 passed in Congress.

It was also the year a hard-driving yet compassionate man named Drew Oosterbaan came to D.C. and to the Child Exploitation Obscenity Section (CEOS), part of the criminal division of the Department of Justice.

Drew Oosterbaan began his career at CEOS as Deputy Chief in January 2000, and by the end of 2001 he was Chief. At that time, the federal government was doing little to nothing to prosecute crimes against children exploited in the sex industry. Under Drew's leadership, CEOS would forge remarkable change.

In these years, my focus broadened and expanded again and again as more information came to light. We researched and compiled the U.S. Midterm Review on Commercial Sexual Exploitation of Children in the United States and the *National Report on Domestic Child Sex Trafficking* — stunning revelations. Other people had been waking up to the issue of child sex trafficking in our nation, and as Shared Hope took part in researching and compiling data working with ECPAT-USA and the Protection Project of Johns Hopkins University, among others, we were waking up just ahead of the rest of the U.S. Into this first decade of the new millennium, the dark underbelly of trafficking in the United States would finally be seen and slowly believed by a shocked public.

In 2010, Drew spoke words that made a huge impact on me and on the future of Shared Hope International. He didn't have any idea that his opinion would be so influential and turn our efforts in a way that has impacted every state in the Union ...

***

I wasn't really interested in the job.

I came to CEOS by circumstance, not by purposeful design. For ten years I'd been an Assistant United States Attorney in Miami, Florida, handling and supervising some of the most interesting and impactful cases in the federal system. I loved Miami, but my wife didn't. So, we decided to pull up stakes and move to Washington, D.C., with our five-year-old son.

In Washington, I was initially on detail as a Trial Attorney to the U.S. Department of Justice Criminal Division's Narcotics and Dangerous Drugs Section, and I was there for only a couple of weeks when the opportunity arose to interview for the position of Deputy Chief of the Child Exploitation and Obscenity Section (CEOS). I wasn't especially experienced in prosecuting federal crimes against children. I had supervised the prosecution of some child pornography cases in Miami, but we were prosecuting every kind of crime. If I had a special expertise in Miami, it was probably centered around violent street crime. While I was moved by the victimization of children, as most people are, I had not seen a particularly significant role taken by federal law enforcement against the sexual exploitation of children. So I was unsure that CEOS was playing a substantial role, and I was afraid that I would be unsatisfied

1987 CEOS

What is CEOS?

The Child Exploitation and Obscenity Section is part of the criminal division of the United States Justice Department. It was created in 1987 with the mission "to protect the welfare of America's children and communities by enforcing federal criminal statutes relating to exploitation of children and obscenity." (https://www.justice.gov// criminal-ceos) with the work there. When it was offered, I decided to take the Deputy Chief job at CEOS anyway, mostly because I wanted to supervise prosecutions again, of any kind.

But once at CEOS, my perspective changed. While I was correct in my perception that at that time CEOS and federal law enforcement had an undersized role in the fight against the sexual exploitation of children, I realized there was much that could be done. The trafficking of children for sex and the market for imagery of child sexual abuse were crime problems growing and worsening at an extremely alarming rate, but these problems were largely unaddressed by federal law enforcement. The reasons for this were clear to me. Law enforcement agencies in the United States and, indeed, internationally are scattered and decentralized. It can be difficult to focus enforcement efforts on crimes that cross borders. Nevertheless, I saw opportunities and, most importantly, a will among many in federal law enforcement to take advantage of them.

Between the two crime problems ripe for federal law enforcement — child sex trafficking and the trafficking of child sexual abuse imagery — child sex trafficking would prove to be the more difficult to address. When I first came to CEOS, sex trafficking was being discussed earnestly at the political level in D.C., but the focus was the international sex trafficking of adults, not children, and not trafficking strictly within the United States. The discussion was often conflated with illegal migration issues, and the truth of victimization was often lost in the political discourse. The subject of international trafficking was getting a lot of attention on Capitol Hill because of strong anti-trafficking advocacy. It was an easy political issue that allowed politicians to be compassionate. But the advocacy and political conversation rarely included child trafficking, and, astonishingly, never included the sex trafficking of American kids.

Back then, if sex trafficking of American children was discussed at all, it was described as "child prostitution," and that vernacular gave the crime a distinctly negative flavor. The term suggested willingness, not victimization, and perhaps a crime not worthy of attention. There was no public or political outcry for these children. Among political and governmental bodies, there was no understanding of this kind of victimization, and no real pressure was felt to change that condition. I thought, *If our own Department of Justice didn't understand what a huge problem we had in the United States, how could anyone else?*

With this as a backdrop, my first year at CEOS as Deputy Chief for Litigation was deeply frustrating. I was in charge of prosecutions, and there just weren't enough of them. I wasn't in a position to set enforcement and prosecution policies. So, by the time the position of Chief at CEOS came open late in 2000, I wasn't inclined to apply.

I did have impactful ideas, however, and lots of them. Therefore, when the newly appointed Chief of the Department's Criminal Division asked me to apply and then interview for the CEOS Chief position, I went ahead and did so. But because I had staked my candidacy on my vision for CEOS, I knew that my selection was an endorsement of this vision. This would prove to be enormously important.

And we had our work cut out for us.

Sex trafficking of U.S. children was a major problem across the country, but, as I've already suggested, a well-kept secret.

Additionally, the market for photos and videos depicting child sexual abuse was a growing pandemic. Together, these issues presented a serious threat to children everywhere, but, tragically, this fact was unappreciated or grossly misunderstood. Nothing would change unless and until this difficult reality was more widely recognized and accepted for the broad risk it posed for children — all children. So one of our first plans of action was to push this dark reality to the forefront. We had to force the topics of child sexual abuse imagery and child sex trafficking into consciousness at the Justice Department and into enforcement policy conversations everywhere.

There was a new administration and a new outlook at the U.S. Department of Justice, and, thankfully, the leadership quickly grasped the nature of the problems and was open to fresh and assertive approaches. They also saw the potential benefit in raising awareness outside the Department. To accomplish this, we started revealing the hidden world of child sexual exploitation, in frank terms, in interviews with print and broadcast media and at public policy conferences. Our purpose was to introduce a broad spectrum of people to the hidden horrors of child sexual exploitation and the risk posed by the growing epidemic, because we knew this would move policy and legislation. And while our conversations were stark, they were also very careful.

Today it is not uncommon to hear politicians and government officials talk about child sex trafficking, child sexual abuse imagery, and other forms of child sexual exploitation. At that time, however, the problems and threats about which I spoke were unseen and almost completely unknown by the public and by legislators and other government officials who were in a position to effect positive change.

Our public conversation about child sexual abuse was not intended to spotlight the work of any particular office, including CEOS, although I'm sure it did that to some extent. We spoke publicly about our work in the belief that appropriate resources would be directed at the problems once people really grasped what was happening and the threats to children posed by these things. I think we were right. Things started changing in a big way.

The decision to make public the horrors of child exploitation was not without potentially dire consequences, however. When it came to statements to the media, we had to weigh the importance of telling people what was happening against the possibility that it might cause further harm to the victimized children. The words we chose were careful and deliberate. The stories told needed to have an impact, but not at any risk that the victims, whose horrors were the subject of our words, would ever feel that impact in a harmful way. This can be difficult, and people who speak in official capacities about child sexual abuse are not always as cognizant of victim interests as they should be.

Examples of this are many. A newspaper can run a story about a young child victimized by sexual abuse that does not name or specifically identify the victim, and the victim could still be re-victimized by the story in a number of different ways. Sometimes the very facts of the story can inadvertently identify the victim to others aware of these facts and subject her to ongoing reputational trauma. Even when the story leaves the identity of the young victim truly hidden, the victim himself may be exposed to the news story, even years after it was published, and re-victimized by it. He may learn things from the media account he never knew or had suppressed, and these things can cause pain felt for the rest of his life.

In addition, these media stories have a never-ending life on the Internet. Given the serious gravity of these possibilities, we had to ensure that our work with the media and the public had the impact on policy-makers we desired while carefully preserving the deeply sensitive interests of the victims whose personal horror we were exposing to influence them. I think we accomplished this. I truly hope we did.

In my early days as Chief of CEOS, I saw the very real and positive impact of raising awareness. One important impact was an increase in specialized investigative and prosecutorial resources dedicated to addressing child sexual exploitation. The most prolific and dangerous offenders used the Internet and advances in technology to gain access to children and hide their identity. Identifying these offenders and stopping them required investigative technology and expertise that previously had not been available in the fight against child sexual exploitation. When such resources were eventually given and leveraged against Internet-facilitated child sexual abuse, the dark corners of the Internet were exposed, rocks were overturned, and these previously anonymous offenders were brought to justice.

Individual investigators and prosecutors did none of this on their own. Relationships and combined efforts are very important in this work, particularly because the offenses we most wanted to address were committed on the borderless Internet. Individual effort and innovation are important, of course, but no one person or entity will ever conceive of the one best way to save or protect children from sexual abuse, although we may sometimes want to believe that we have. The problem is just too big, too complex, and too dynamic. In my experience, where true success was achieved, more often than not, it was the result of a whole lot of people working together with common purpose and without regard for credit. Every major internet-based operation we successfully conducted involved countless dedicated investigators from agencies around the world working tirelessly in concert to identify offenders and save their child victims. When one agency acts alone to address an online community of offenders, they always fail at some level, and child victims around the world remain suffering in perpetual anonymity as a result.

Meaningful connection between investigators and academics is also very important. I was fortunate to learn this early on, and the lesson served me well throughout my time at CEOS. Investigators tend to view offending one dimensionally: it's criminal behavior. But a deeper understanding of the issues involved in child sexual exploitation is critically important to understanding how to address the issues effectively. Many of the most important advances during my time at CEOS were realized when professionals from outside law enforcement — researchers, academics, or technology experts, for instance — shared their insight and expertise with law enforcement agencies, and these agencies were accepting.

Unfortunately, this kind of sharing was exceedingly rare in the early 2000s. Law enforcement generally saw these kinds of relationships as unnecessary, actually, if not adversarial. In my early days at CEOS, I didn't see the full value in such exchanges either. But this changed for me once and forever as a result of a chance meeting and a single conversation. The impact was enormous, at least from my point of view.

The conversation took place in the margins of a conference dedicated to cross-border issues between Canada and the United States held in Vancouver, British Columbia, in October 2000. I made a presentation at the conference as part of a panel on the topic of child sexual abuse images on the Internet. Also on the panel was Dr. Max Taylor.

Dr. Taylor was a professor and head of the Department of Applied Psychology at University College Cork in Ireland. While teaching psychology, Max created the Child Studies Unit (CSU) that sought to help kids in conflict zones through research, training, and policy development. He also formed the COPINE Project (Combating Paedophile Information Networks in Europe). COPINE was funded by the EU and worked with the London Metro Police and Scotland Yard's Paedophile Unit.

The COPINE team at the university was searching for and downloading images of child sexual abuse from internet newsgroups, cataloging them, and then providing them to law enforcement in England as evidence of the crimes depicted in the images and with hope that the victim would be identified and found. At the same time, new case law in the U.S. required prosecutors to prove that the child depicted in sexual abuse imagery was a real child, and the subject of image databases to aid in this proof was of growing interest. It occurred to me that Dr. Taylor's efforts in cataloging child abuse images might just be the beginning of the database I thought we needed.

I spoke to Max about my database ideas and suggested to him that a comprehensive catalog of images would serve the critical purpose of proving the child in the image is a real child. But he stopped me.

"Databases," he said. "I keep hearing people talk about databases, but we're missing the point."

Max told me about this team at the university and how they had volunteer students looking at these horrible images not just to catalog information about them, but to look for clues to identify and locate the kids. They would search the photographic and video images for anything that might reveal a city, region, or even country — information that could be an important step toward finding these kids and stopping the abuse.

And they'd been successful. COPINE had shared information with law enforcement in London, and the police were able to locate and rescue several young girls. Not surprisingly, this success was having a profound effect on the officers involved too. One officer who was in the very first rescue would end up spending the rest of his career doing the same work.

As I listened to Dr. Taylor, I saw his point easily. It's hard to imagine now, because today the approach is vastly different and victim identification is an overwhelmingly common law enforcement practice in investigations involving child sex abuse images. But it wasn't at that time. Back then, law enforcement agencies were focused almost exclusively on putting offenders in jail and did not view child sexual abuse imagery as the crime scene evidence it was. Investigators generally saw the children depicted in sexual abuse images as anonymous victims, and rarely, if ever, used the images to find them. My thought had been to use comprehensive databases of child abuse images to facilitate prosecution, not necessarily rescue

1998

COPINE (Combating Paedophile Information Networks in Europe) Project and Scale

The COPINE Scale categorized child abuse images in a 10-level typology based on the analyses of the images. The range started at *Indicative*, which were non-sexual images yet because of their collection may indicate some sexual interest in children. The Scale's 10th category included *Sadistic*. This scale was used to hunt for pedophiles and the evidence was used in court cases against them. The COPINE Scale was formed through the COPINE Project by Professor Max Taylor and the staff at the Department of Applied Psychology, University College Cork, Ireland.[1]

victims. The difference, of course, was enormous. While getting convictions was essential, Max was talking about rescuing the children. Max was right — we were missing the point.

Listening to Max changed my perspective profoundly, and I returned to my office in D.C. with a much better plan. Some big changes were necessary. We needed to build a database, but it would be used to save children as well as for prosecutions.

As I've mentioned, the most significant law enforcement success in this area was built on selfless teamwork. But that doesn't mean that teams were easily created and directed. Building the right teams was difficult then, and it likely still is, unfortunately. Given this reality, I learned early in my tenure to convene the federal law enforcement agencies with jurisdiction over child exploitation crimes at the National Center for Missing and Exploited Children. I enjoyed a very good working relationship with Ernie Allen, and we often had similar viewpoints. Ernie is truly a visionary in the realm of child protection, and his enormous impact within that realm was unprecedented at the time and, in my view, is unequalled since. Ernie was well aware of the sensitivities and difficulties involved in developing common law enforcement policy among the many federal law enforcement entities.

As a former prosecutor himself, he also knew that CEOS, a section of federal prosecutors, served a role between all of them. We were natural allies, and we often held federal law enforcement meetings together at the neutral territory that NCMEC offered. Ernie was in complete agreement on the necessity to create a database to find and save children, as well as to facilitate prosecutions. We both knew that NCMEC was the only place that could create and sustain the kind of apparatus required for this. However, the notion of a database of illegal images held and operated by a non-law enforcement, indeed non-governmental organization, was completely unheard of at the time. This notion also was not easy for the federal law enforcement agencies to accept, particularly because some of them could reasonably claim the right and ability to take on the responsibility. To work this out, Ernie and I called a series of meetings at NCMEC.

The conversations were not easy. The agencies saw the importance of the database, even if they would not see its full and true value in identifying victims for some time to come. Nevertheless, I can say with sincerity that as these meetings progressed I saw the kind of selfless cooperation that would be the hallmark of investigative successes in the future. More significantly, these meetings represented the first time the major federal law enforcement agencies in the U.S. meaningfully discussed the requirement to identify the victims depicted in child sexual abuse imagery and common approaches to finding them. We talked about the necessary investments and the roles we all would play, including

2002

CEOS and the High Technology Investigative Unit

The High Technology Investigative Unit (HTIU) would become the experts in prosecuting child exploitation cases and investigating high-technology child exploitation crimes.

CEOS attorneys and HTIU computer forensic specialists seek to blend investigative and prosecutorial experience with policy expertise in order to create innovative solutions to the threats posed by those who violate federal child exploitation laws.

the primary and essential role of NCMEC. Progress was not easy, but Ernie, NCMEC, and law enforcement leaders around the table at these meetings committed to achieving success, and from then forward never wavered from that goal. And although we weren't quite sure what success would look like then, we all knew the law enforcement community dedicated to addressing crimes against children would never be the same. Thankfully, we were completely right about that.

That group of leaders mapped an approach that we informally called the Victim Identification Program (VIP), with the National Center for Missing and Exploited Children serving its primary operational functions. Over the ensuing years, VIP evolved into a massive-scale, highly coordinated, and supremely effective mechanism involving the National Center, law enforcement across the country and around the globe, and countless private companies working in the internet service industry. The success of this program can be measured in the astounding number of victims identified and the truly impressive and heartwarming number of children found and saved.

But I will always be proud of the broader impact of the

effort we started with those meetings at NCMEC. Child victim identification is now a paramount principle of law enforcement worldwide. Federal, state, and local law enforcement agencies across the United States have units dedicated to searching images and videos of child sexual abuse for clues that might help establish the identity and whereabouts of the victim depicted in the imagery. These units are closely networked and share the information and clues they develop with fellow officers around the world who work in a common effort to save children.

***

Drew's work as Chief of CEOS continued to see great results, but there were some big challenges ahead that might have changed everything in the fight to save kids. When we invade the darkness, there is never a time to turn back …

---

[1] Academic Dictionaries and Encyclopedias, http://enacademic.com/dic.nsf/enwiki/11577639.

11

JUSTICE AT WORK

Drew Oosterbaan

"WHEN YOU COME DOWN TO IT, IT'S REALLY ONE PROBLEM — A PREVALENT SEXUAL INTEREST IN CHILDREN."

DREW OOSTERBAAN

In many ways, the Internet explosion exposed the problem of child sexual abuse in new light. As the Internet took hold and our investigative work began to catch up with the technology, we saw a massive population of individuals demonstrating a sexual interest in children. Before the Internet, these people were isolated and hidden from each other. In common public perception, a predilection for sex with children is condemnable. Given this perception, those with a sexual interest in children, whether acted upon or not, certainly do not reveal that interest publicly. Indeed, before the Internet I think it is fair to say that many, if not most, people with this unlawful penchant saw themselves as somehow deranged and unlike anyone else. In this feeling there was isolation and deterrence. Then the Internet came along, and pretty quickly people with deviant interests, like sex between adults and children, began to find each other there, and in vast numbers. They found normalcy online, because they saw for the first time that their sexual interest in children was far from unique. For the first time, their sexual desires felt not all that abnormal.

The Internet also connected such people in nurturing ways. In their online relationships with compatible people, they found encouragement, normalization, and justification. The Internet revolutionized the lives of those who desired sex with children, both because of the legitimacy they could rationalize for themselves within the community of like-mindedness found there and the amazingly effective vehicle it provided for following through on their perverse interests.

As with most things online, individual connections led to newsgroups, message boards, forums, and communities dedicated to the sexual abuse of children. These groups and communities grew exponentially, with worldwide membership sometimes in the tens of thousands. And while the common interest of members was child sexual abuse, the currency that truly bound them together was imagery; images and videos of children being sexually abused. Child sexual abuse imagery was and still is a commodity for those who convene over child sexual abuse on the Internet. Providing child sexual abuse images to these groups is how newly subscribing members prove they belong and gain acceptance, and members who can provide fresh or more deviant images, which are more valuable to the membership, are exalted by the community.

Indeed, the prize to members of a community dedicated to the sexual abuse of children is to have images of sexual abuse that have never before been seen, either because the victim or the abuse is new. Many groups had tiers. If someone wanted to rise into a more elite part of the group, the member had to produce images. If you didn't have a new image of a child, you were likely to be ignored. If you could produce new images or videos, however, you were heralded, rewarded, with promotion to special status in the group. This, of course, is a huge incentive for members to get access to a vulnerable child — a child in their own home, a neighbor, a prostituted child — and create an opportunity to abuse that child while capturing the abuse in imagery.

In my view, the Internet and the truly wonderful vehicle for communication that it is can place children everywhere at greater risk.

Unfortunately, it is very difficult to infiltrate this dark world.

The technology used to commit these crimes presented big challenges. The members of groups and communities dedicated to the sexual abuse of children and exchanging imagery of it were, and still are, early adopters of advanced internet technology. As technology moved forward, people who would abuse it for criminal purposes did as well, and very quickly. Among other things, they found and mastered ways to maintain their anonymity when conducting illegal activity, such as exchanging child sexual abuse imagery. As time and technology progressed, investigators found it difficult to keep pace.

In the early days, we often developed evidence of the distribution of illegal imagery, used the evidence to get a warrant and seize the hard drive from the person who received the images, but then find ourselves unable to prove the identity of the person responsible for the original distribution of the images — the source. Investigations frequently ended with proof against only the end possessor of the images, which was good, but not good enough. An additional problem was that even in the most successful investigations, resulting prosecutions could be lost because the technology involved was very difficult to explain to juries.

To address these problems, I created the High Technology Investigative Unit within CEOS in 2002. This in-house unit was comprised of digital technology specialists and federal law enforcement agents who worked closely with CEOS prosecutors to develop highly effective strategies targeting online child sexual abuse imagery networks (sometimes referred to as *child pornography* networks), typically uncovering large-scale sexual abuse of children. These experts knew the technology and the methodology used by offenders to employ it inside and out. Just as significantly, they also knew how to explain these concepts to a jury of everyday citizens who could only be stunned by the explanations. We could get to the source of the illegal images and then successfully prosecute him in court.

The idea for the unit was mine, but it was built by someone else. He was the perfect architect, and I had to hire him first. He knew the technology, and because he had been working as a consultant for the unit at U.S. Customs investigating online crime, he was thoroughly versed in how child sex abusers were using the Internet to successfully commit their crimes. We enticed him from that highly lucrative consulting role to a relatively poor-paying government job with the only thing we could offer: the opportunity to save children. Thankfully, that's all he wanted. From then on, CEOS and the federal law enforcement community with which we worked were never again short-sided in the fight against child sexual offending online. We were on our way to establishing a force of investigators from law enforcement agencies around the world, fully equipped to reveal and prosecute the most prolific, insidious, and dangerous offenders on the planet.

With the success of the HTIU and growing interest among decision-makers at the Department of Justice, the tide turned in favor of prosecution of offenses involving child sexual abuse imagery. Widespread understanding of the size and significance of the threat posed by the online exchange of this imagery emerged, as did a structure for successful law enforcement over the long term. Indeed, once successful prosecutions of high-impact offenders began to increase, I saw an unprecedented level of support at the Department for law enforcement programs focused on child protection. Eventually, this support and interest would include enforcement against child sex trafficking, but that took a little more time.

Strong departmental interest in child sex trafficking developed after we initiated a project that eventually became known as the Innocence Lost National Initiative. This idea developed somewhat organically, in meetings and conversations with Ernie Allen at NCMEC and

2003 INNOCENCE LOST INITIATIVE

The Innocence Lost Initiative is a joint initiative between the FBI, the U.S. Justice Department's Child Exploitation and Obscenity Section (CEOS), and the National Center for Missing and Exploited Children (NCMEC) that targeted child prostitution in the United States. It was the first federal initiative of its kind.

with an agent at the FBI named Eileen Jacobs.

The combination of CEOS, NCMEC, and the FBI was an ideal confluence of forces against child sex trafficking. Much of the credit for the ideas that became Innocence Lost belongs to Ernie Allen and Eileen Jacobs, who had long been strong advocates for focused law enforcement approaches against the prostitution of minors. From their days in Kentucky, Ernie Allen and John Rabun had long championed a multi-disciplinary approach to addressing the problem. In my position, I hoped to be able to shape the project into something that would get financial support and effectual backing at the Department.

Ernie and I started talking about developing the initiative in 2002. In addition to its place as a powerful NGO that made things happen in Washington, NCMEC had been providing training to state and local law enforcement for many years. We wanted to create task forces in cities and towns around the country specifically trained to address child sex trafficking, and NCMEC would be the ideal vehicle for this training.

Ernie's experience in Kentucky had convinced him that the key to success against child sex trafficking was putting the variety of independent resources with a stake in the problem together in one common approach. That is, street-level investigators, victim service providers, and prosecutors had to work in tandem. This would be completely novel to the investigators, providers, and prosecutors who had to effectuate the approach. As such, we knew that training was key. We wanted social service practitioners, law enforcement officers, and prosecutors from the same local areas to train together in teams or task forces. We wanted them to learn together and plan together in order to address the problem together. So we sat down and created a training agenda and staffed the faculty with experts in child sex trafficking enforcement and victim services. Then, with NCMEC funding reallocated from other areas, the National Center began bringing multi-disciplinary teams from around the country to its training facility for a week-long training program. This approach had a momentous and enduring impact on sex-trafficking enforcement.

At the same time, I sent CEOS prosecutors to U.S. Attorney's Offices across the country to meet with federal, state, and local practitioners. With no formal mandate or special funding, these CEOS prosecutors from Washington traveled to a large number of cities in different parts of the U.S. and brought together the same types of practitioners NCMEC was bringing in for training. Their purpose was to raise awareness of the problem of child sex trafficking and generate movement toward the establishment of multi-disciplinary teams or task forces and local enforcement programs. The people the CEOS prosecutors brought together did not necessarily think they needed assistance from Washington, and they certainly weren't asking for it, so this was no easy task.

For their part, the FBI made child sex trafficking a national priority. This meant that FBI agents around the country who investigated violent crime would prioritize child sex trafficking over other types of criminal investigations. FBI agents also joined in NCMEC training, both as trainers and trainees, and they joined with CEOS prosecutors in local efforts to initiate local enforcement activities.

The Innocence Lost Initiative began without any new funding, and it was designed to be self-sustaining regardless of funding. The initiative moved forward with great success for many years before the FBI was able to finance it directly, and it continues successfully with substantial funding today.

Did it turn out exactly as it was envisioned? It didn't, but it is not unusual for major law enforcement initiatives to begin with one set of plans and then evolve to a different, finished product. The emphasis on multi-disciplinary training and task forces may have diminished, but the enforcement methodology at the core of Innocence Lost has become so well entrenched that such training has become less critical. Regardless, the success of our early efforts is seen in the enduring emphasis on victim-centered approaches to addressing child sex trafficking, even if victim services are not always part of enforcement planning.

Perhaps the best measure of our early impact, however, is the enormous increase in prosecutions. In 2002 we saw very few. Today, the number of federal and state sex trafficking prosecutions every year is large and impressive. Innocence Lost is now a well-funded, thoroughly entrenched program at the FBI. Child sex trafficking enforcement and rescuing trafficking victims is a priority around the country and, indeed, around the world. I could not imagine in 2002 that I would ever see this kind of impact and growth, and I'd like to think our early work had something to do with the current condition.

By 2005, the Innocence Lost Initiative was in full motion, and our successful efforts in combatting the trafficking of child sexual abuse imagery and in victim identification was widely known and appreciated at the Department of Justice. Senior leadership was eager to expand on this success and further prioritize child protection. I took advantage of this willingness to expand the scope of the work already in progress in every way possible. However, while the emphasis on enforcement had been growing, so had the sophistication, connectivity, and proliferation of the offenders. The egregiousness of the images and videos we were seeing continued to worsen as well, which we attributed to the demand for such imagery. And, of course, the technology abused by the offenders to commit their crimes against children was advancing at a breakneck pace.

We had to get even better at what we were doing. We had to double down on our enforcement commitment and increase the resources dedicated to investigating child sexual abuse offenses. While CEOS often worked with specialized federal law enforcement units at the headquarters level to address child exploitation, most of the relatively limited enforcement resources available to address the rampant problem of child sexual exploitation online were scattered around the country, working largely in isolation. If we could organize and better leverage these independent resources, we could do so much more, but changing the mentality feeding the condition of independence would be akin to changing a system of government. These were law enforcement entities, federal, state, and local, that enjoyed their independence, and rightfully so. To all of the people involved, it was seen simply as the way things had to be.

The resulting effort to organize the totality of online child protection resources around the United States was the most significant and comprehensive law enforcement initiative ever undertaken against online child sexual exploitation in the United States. It was called Project Safe Childhood, and it began in 2006.

CEOS was heavily involved in the planning and

implementation of the Attorney General's Project Safe Childhood (PSC) initiative, which became the Department's keynote policy and operational initiative to combat child exploitation online. The overall strategy was meant to fully coordinate and focus the disparate resources around the country involved in addressing child exploitation crimes facilitated on the Web. One of PSC's most significant features was the development and implementation of the Project Safe Childhood Regional Team Trainings. I borrowed this concept from our Innocence Lost Initiative. These trainings brought together teams consisting of a federal prosecutor, federal agents, and investigators from the more than 1,800 local law enforcement agencies that were members or affiliates of the 59 Internet Crimes Against Children (ICAC) task forces. The trainings were conducted regionally around the country, and hundreds of federal, state, and local prosecutors and investigators participated. CEOS developed and fulfilled the training agenda for this program, which was designed to train state and local investigators to investigate the most sophisticated and high-impact Internet-facilitated child exploitation offenses and bring them to federal prosecutors for successful federal prosecution.

The improvements wrought by PSC were substantial. For example, the program resulted in a large increase in cases investigated by state and local investigators and prosecuted in federal court, where sentencing features at the time typically resulted in stiffer penalties than in state courts. Additionally, international operations targeting online communities of child sexual abuse image traffickers were handled far more effectively. Previously, an operation would develop preliminary evidence against hundreds of offenders in the United

States, but due to the inadequacy of available resources within the lead federal agency, only a relatively small number of these offenders ended up in prosecution. The initiative ensured that a far greater number of leads from these high-impact international child pornography operations were fully investigated, resulting in a far greater number of successful prosecutions.

Initially, Project Safe Childhood focused exclusively on the trading of child abuse imagery and identifying the victims. The initiative did not incorporate the Innocence Lost Initiative, which focused on child sex trafficking. It took several years of my urging, but eventually the focus of Project Safe Childhood was expanded to include Internet-facilitated child sex trafficking. This was important, as PSC was a priority for the Department of Justice, and this meant federal prosecutors were committed to accomplish its goals. Adding child sex trafficking to PSC ensured that the work of the Innocence Lost task forces and other resources focused on child sex trafficking

2006

PROJECT SAFE CHILDHOOD

Project Safe Childhood is a unified and comprehensive strategy to combat child exploitation led by the U.S. Attorneys' Office and CEOS. Federal, state, and local resources are used to identify and rescue child victims and to apprehend and prosecute perpetrators who sexually exploited children.

The goal of Project Safe Childhood is to reduce the incidence of sexual exploitation of children. There are five essential components to Project Safe Childhood: (1) building partnerships; (2) coordinating law enforcement; (3) training PSC partners; (4) public awareness; and (5) accountability.

would get the attention from prosecutors it deserved.

I no longer track the number of traffickers convicted and children recovered under Project Safe Childhood and Innocence Lost, although I am sure the statistics have been published by the Department of Justice and the FBI. Nevertheless, I know the impact these initiatives have made, and it is enormous and enduring.

Under PSC, child exploitation enforcement became a true and meaningful priority. Large and specialized resource commitments were made and not reversed, which is not always the case with crime initiatives. Victim-centered approaches became the norm. A career investigating or prosecuting crimes against children became not only possible but coveted. Firm and lasting partnerships between federal and state law enforcement agencies were established. Specialized units employing effective investigative techniques focusing on finding and saving victims were developed and took hold. With the strong demand PSC produced, industry giants like Facebook and Google created special teams of analysts within their compliance sections to reveal and report crimes against children committed on their systems and to respond to law enforcement officers investigating these crimes. The initiative removed or substantially reduced every remaining impediment. Its success is truly exceptional — and largely irreversible.

Interestingly enough, however, the fate of PSC and child exploitation enforcement may have been much different but for a meeting I had with the U.S. Attorney General in early 2005. I will not speak here for the Attorney General, but I believe he initially intended this meeting to be my last as Chief of CEOS.

In February 2005, the President appointed a new Attorney

General of the United States. When top departmental leadership changes, many things can change, and sometimes people lose their jobs. I knew well that there were politically powerful people who wanted me out as Chief of CEOS. These people wanted CEOS to focus its prosecutorial effort on "obscenity," or illegal adult pornography, and not on child sexual exploitation. CEOS had responsibility for prosecuting both, but for reasons that were obvious to me, child exploitation crimes were our clear priority.

However, there were strong and influential voices pushing for more obscenity prosecutions because they felt this would have a positive societal impact. These people also frequently conflated the dangers presented by child sexual abuse images and child sex trafficking with the societal issues presented by adult pornography, arguing — speciously, in my view — that abundance and availability of adult pornography was the root cause of child sexual exploitation. This argument was convincing to some. Many of these people thought I was to blame for deemphasizing obscenity enforcement (and perhaps for the overall decay of society, as well), and some with political connections used whatever influence they could muster to achieve my removal as the Chief of CEOS.

They were not entirely wrong in blaming me — at least for the emphasis on addressing child sexual exploitation over obscenity. CEOS was certainly very focused on addressing child sexual abuse, child sex trafficking, and the trafficking of child sexual abuse images during my years as Chief, and it still is. It will surprise no one who knows me or who was part of CEOS at the time that I am completely unapologetic about this.

Soon after the appointment of the new Attorney General,

I was told by members of the Criminal Division front office that he had met with some of the people who sought my ouster and now wanted to meet with me. (It should be noted here that while the position of Section Chief within the Criminal Division is a senior executive management position, it sits at a level low enough within the hierarchical order that a visit from the U.S. Attorney General is exceedingly rare. The Attorney General doesn't come to you — you go to the Attorney General. His visit to my office so soon after his appointment suggested to me clearly that his agenda for me was not routine. The political appointees directly above me knew this as well. I was certain he was coming to fire me, unless I could convince him not to.)

When I told the CEOS management team about the visit, they also knew what was at stake. It should not be difficult to imagine the pall this placed over the section. CEOS members had worked exceptionally hard and had earned significant and meaningful success. If the AG removed me, it would feel to them like a rejection of all they had accomplished.

The stated reason for the AG's visit, however, was to receive a briefing about the work of CEOS. This meant that I would have at least a small opportunity to highlight our efforts to address child sexual abuse and exploitation. Because these efforts had been formidable and the results impressive, I decided that if I was to be removed, I'd leave only after showing him everything we were doing at CEOS to protect children and why. It was the why that was most important.

Crimes against children in any form are condemnable. This precept stands on its own. But anyone who investigates or prosecutes child sexual abuse crimes knows that there is one sure way to convince the uninitiated that the trafficking of child sexual abuse is worthy of aggressive enforcement effort: you need only show them some of the photos and videos of children being raped that are habitually exchanged online. I told my team, "I'm going to show him images."

As Chief, I had no need to look at child sexual abuse images or videos, and I didn't. It had not been since I was the supervisor of line prosecutors many years earlier that I experienced child sexual abuse images. So, as I was about to prepare a PowerPoint briefing for the AG, I asked the Director of our High Technology Investigative Unit to provide me with a few examples. He did, but when I saw them, I knew I couldn't use them as I had planned. I couldn't show the U.S. Attorney General images that I knew, once seen, would haunt him endlessly. These images, and the videos especially, are permanently scarring. Perhaps he would never fully appreciate our focus on children and he might fire me, but I wasn't going to do that to him.

Instead, I decided to choose another means to ensure that he understood, as deeply as possible, what we were fighting against and why our efforts were entirely worthwhile. We created one special slide. It was a collage of faces of victimized children. They were cropped from the images I had decided not to show him fully — just faces.

On the morning of the meeting I was anxious, so I went down to the lobby early to wait for him. I hoped my immediate supervisors, who I felt had my back, would get there a bit early so that I could take them through the outline of my briefing and perhaps gain some confidence. As I walked out of the lobby elevators, however, I saw the Attorney General and an entourage of about five people enter the building. The Attorney General was a full 15 minutes early. My front office hadn't even arrived yet. It was just me.

We greeted each other without pleasantries and then headed for the elevator. As we ascended the six floors to where CEOS was housed, not a single word was spoken. It was truly one of the most awkward moments of my life, standing in that elevator with a group of people I believed were set on removing me from my job, not a single one of them looking at or speaking to me.

Once in my office, my efforts to delay until the Chief of the Criminal Division arrived were unavailing. I tried to make small talk, but no one was talking. Faces were serious and, from my perspective, unfriendly. There was little else I could do but offer to start the briefing. The AG quickly agreed.

We went into the conference room and because it was still prior to the scheduled start time, it was empty. I was trying to open my own PowerPoint when the Attorney General said, "Drew, a lot of people care about obscenity. Do you care?"

I looked at him and said, "Yes, I do. But I care about a lot of the things we do at CEOS, and I plan to tell you about all of them."

I started the presentation with only the AG and his staff in attendance. I began with obscenity, because I knew that is what he wanted to hear about. That didn't take long. In short order, I talked about the truly impactful and unprecedented progress we were making against child exploitation. This should have been an exultant moment for me, but the looks on the faces of the group from the AG's office denied me that. Then, the officially scheduled time for the briefing arrived, and the space behind the Attorney General filled up with CEOS staff — the people who were doing all of the great work against child sexual exploitation I had just begun to describe. In that moment of realization, I forgot about the grim reasons the AG might have for coming and just felt an enormous sense of responsibility. I was speaking for the people of CEOS. I was speaking for all of their work and its legacy. From that moment forward, I was only exhilarated.

As the briefing continued, there was a change in the AG's temperament, and in the others in his group, as well. I described our international investigative operations, unprecedented in scope and accomplishment, our hopeful successes in child victim identification, our hard work to create and initiate the Innocence Lost task forces that were spreading around the country, and the critical advances in law enforcement enabled by CEOS's High Technology Investigative Unit. I provided statistics and numbers to support all of these efforts. Each slide and every word told the impressive story of achievement of all the people sitting behind the Attorney General. And when the special slide hit the screen, I am sure the AG was powerfully gripped by the faces of those children — children who were being identified and saved through our efforts. I told him that I had planned to show him the full images. I described some of the horror the imagery depicts and explained my reason for not showing them to him. As I described the images, the AG and his group shook their heads unconsciously, and it was clear they understood.

At the end of my presentation, the Attorney General stood up. I believe he was so taken in by what he saw and heard that he was unaware the room had filled up behind him. He turned and looked for the first time at the CEOS prosecutors and digital analysts. These were the people who were responsible for the great achievement he had just heard me pronounce. They had been traveling around the country, knocking on doors to get child prostitution cases prosecuted. They had been forging paths and relationships to develop the first-ever international operations against the most prolific traffickers in misery that the world knew and seeing to it that these offenders were brought to justice. They had been teaching law enforcement officers and prosecutors around the country how to get convictions that count and to save victims. And, these were the people who had to witness the horrors just described to the AG every working day. Having just heard my presentation, he knew all of this. Perhaps it was an awkward moment for him. If he had indeed come with the intent to fire me, it was because he had been told CEOS wasn't doing enough, and he now knew this was far from true.

He thanked the group and said what they did was important to him and to his wife, which I took as a very personal comment. Then he and his team left, having stayed far longer than was scheduled.

I didn't know what to expect next. What happened, though, surprised me.

The briefing had worked.

One day several months afterward, as I was driving to the job I still had, I got a call from the Attorney General's assistant saying he was coming back to my office later that morning. This time he wanted to see the full images and videos that I hadn't shown him at the first briefing. The next day he would announce a major child protection policy initiative, Project Safe Childhood, and felt he had to witness the abuse firsthand, as the images force you to do, in order to properly capture the horror of them in the speech he was to give.

We loaded a video and some images regularly trafficked in our secure viewing room, and he came to our office and viewed them. I stood behind him and watched him physically recoil, as if he had been struck, when the video played and he heard the screams of the very young girl who was being raped.

A U.S. Attorney General has many critically important priorities. The AG is the chief federal law enforcement officer and carries the requirement to resolve a multitude of pressing and momentous issues. Then, as now, the United States faced serious threats from terrorists, and the Attorney General was managing law enforcement's efforts to thwart them, among many other responsibilities. After that briefing, however, I think it is fair to say that none of the law enforcement issues the Attorney General faced was more important to him, on a personal level, than the prevention of child sexual abuse. During his time as Attorney General, he proved that time and again. A few times during his tenure at the Department of Justice, either in a phone call or in person, the AG would ask me, "Drew, are we doing enough? Should we be doing more?"

Project Safe Childhood was his initiative. I'd like to think he sees it as his signature initiative and the one he cared about most, but it really doesn't matter. I believe he may have been the strongest advocate as

2006

THE U.S. MIDTERM REVIEW

SHI spearheads the U.S. Mid-Term Review bringing together leaders from across the USA to assess progress made combating the sexual slavery of children in America.

U.S. Attorney General for child abuse prevention the Department of Justice has ever known.

I first connected with Shared Hope International through Samantha Vardaman. We met at an event at Johns Hopkins University where Shared Hope had convened professionals from civil society and government agencies to create the CSEC Midterm Review document called for at the CSEC World Congress. I was participating on a panel, talking about the work of the U.S. Department of Justice and CEOS.

Not long after that Johns Hopkins event, Samantha and I met at another anti-sex trafficking event in northwest Washington, D.C. After talking for a while, we discussed how I needed a ride since our location wasn't accessible by public transportation, and taxis were scarce in that area. I was effectively stuck. She agreed to drive me back to my office — along with at least four others packed into her two-door car. I'm sure friendships are often made in such ways.

While CEOS had relationships with a number of NGOs, these relationships were by necessity conducted at arm's length. NGOs like Shared Hope International potentially have a unique and powerful capacity, because they can do certain impactful things that a governmental organization cannot. For instance, they can lobby on the Hill for an issue as befits their purpose and goals. They can ignore political expediency and, more importantly, ignore government policy. Indeed, they can openly and publicly criticize government policy, and the good ones like Shared Hope often do. Many NGOs came up against sex trafficking with good intentions, but often without the knowledge, design, or focused aptitude to make a real impact.

I quickly learned that Shared Hope was an NGO that was making an impact, for many reasons. Samantha, my first contact with the organization, is a lawyer, and she takes nothing for granted. CEOS consists of a group of lawyers, among other specialists, and the lawyers were (and continue to be) bright, talented, and steeped in the law associated with child sexual exploitation. Additionally, CEOS prosecutors work with other prosecutors and investigators on significant cases around the country and have a perspective of real value, framed by the practical and legal issues they deal with as prosecutors. In fact, no governmental entity had more to say about these issues than we did. So if you are responsible for an NGO dedicated to changing the lives of sex-trafficking victims as Samantha and Linda are, it makes sense to listen to CEOS's perspective. And they did.

Before Shared Hope went to the Hill and lobbied for a bill or were part of a hearing, Samantha would often ask of us, "What do you think of this?" I believe she in particular saw benefit in our counsel, and she listened. She was adaptive. The benefits of considering other perspectives seems obvious, I know, but receptiveness of other viewpoints is not always a habit you find in lobbyists and advocates. However, while Samantha frequently sought our position on legislation or case law, she always examined our position against her own research and significant experience. She usually knew the law and the facts as well as we did.

I saw much to like about Shared Hope International. They were effective lobbyists who got information from the right sources. They did excellent research as seen with the Midterm Review and the National Report, and they leveraged it. They targeted demand

— the buyers — when most advocacy groups ignored this important part of the problem. I also saw that while they were a relatively small NGO, they were making a real difference. Over the years, we developed a trust, which is critically important to any relationship, but perhaps rare in relationships between government agencies and NGOs in D.C.

At some point in 2010, Samantha called and asked whether I would meet with her and Linda to discuss ideas. I was happy to oblige, although a meeting with Linda was unusual for me. We met at the Starbucks across the street from my office on the corner of 14th and New York Avenue NW.

I knew they wanted to talk about ideas, but that's all I knew. For some time, Shared Hope had been shifting from a focus on international sex trafficking of women and children to a more direct focus on domestic trafficking of children. They had been successful lobbyists and had done good field training work, but Linda expressed that she wanted to do more. I sensed they were looking for a game-changer in the field. And I'm never short of ideas.

In so many words I said, "Linda, you know how to do this. Use your unique strength. You worked as a lawmaker at the state and federal levels, but you have to take this issue to the local level. You need to change how state and local policy-makers look at prostitution and spur them to action in the streets. They need to see the problem not as trafficking, although it is, but as the abject sexual victimization of children on the streets and in the hotels of their communities. If anyone can make them see this and act on it, you can. And, if you turn the viewpoints of the governors and mayors and city managers, state and local law enforcement will follow because they'll have to."

She didn't appear immediately convinced, but she was thinking about it. I am sure that, sitting there, outside with coffee in hand along a busy street in our nation's capital, the thought of convincing policy-makers in countless local jurisdictions in fifty states, all with different laws, practices, and policies, was daunting. We both knew that most states and localities were ignoring the problem, but it was equally clear that state and local enforcement was important to any progress. This was a local, even street-level, crime for the most part, and federal law enforcement was not positioned to deal with the problem at that level.

Sex trafficking happened in the truck stops, motels, and out on the streets. Yet for local law enforcement, because sex trafficking was seen as prostitution, it was a low priority — maybe the lowest in crime-ridden urban areas. And while it was known that minors were often found among the large number of prostitutes arrested in urban communities, local law enforcement saw this as an intractable, multi-dimensional problem they were not capable of resolving.

Besides, the child victims usually lied about their ages when arrested, and it was an extensive, often fruitless effort to identify them as the minors they were. If police officers did go to their bosses over some girl they were sure was under-age, the response was typically negative: "Forget about that, you've got murders and robberies to focus on. You may think it's an under-age person, but we don't have the time to find out."

Every jurisdiction in every state and county had a different bureaucracy. In any urban area there may be several police authorities. Some jurisdictions position the police chief under the city manager, and the city manager under the mayor. In some areas where local resources were fully stretched, nothing could happen without state resources brought to bear. Figuring out who to influence would be half the battle.

As I expressed to Linda at the Starbucks meeting, however, the key to turning things around was to get the people who controlled the police to see that what they considered to be a prostitution problem they couldn't afford to care about was instead a child exploitation issue they couldn't afford to ignore. Politicians at every level can be convinced to do something to address the sexual abuse of children. What was happening on the streets and in the myriad tawdry locales of our cities was at least equivalent to, if not worse than, the international sex trafficking that politicians in Washington had been addressing for years. This was the domestic sex trafficking of children. Someone needed to make local politicians see prostitution in this way — and that would be Shared Hope.

I claim no credit for convincing Linda of an approach she already understood, but Shared Hope went to work. When and where they could, they trained local officials to understand the dynamics and features of the domestic sex trafficking of children. They created the Protected Innocence Challenge that gave every state in the U.S. a report card on the strength of its laws in the fight against child sex trafficking. These report cards

2010

THE PROTECTED INNOCENCE CHALLENGE

This annual report gives a grade for each state in the USA based on 41 key points of law relating to child sex trafficking. It is the nation's only comprehensive study on state laws on child trafficking. State report cards and grades can be viewed on sharedhope.org.

are now given out every year. With this measure to motivate them, over the years, states have improved their scores to a commendable degree. This was an important change, and it was desperately needed. Shared Hope made that change happen, and it was yet another critically significant turning point.

I remained at CEOS until 2015. I am exceedingly proud to have served as Chief of that section, to have worked with such dedicated and talented professionals, and to have been part of real and impactful change. The Department of Justice does some of its best work through criminal division sections like CEOS, where prosecutors and digital forensic analysts handle the most significant investigations, prosecutions, and enforcement initiatives around the country and then use the knowledge and expertise gained through to influence law enforcement policy and legislative frameworks.

***

That conversation at Starbucks with Drew incited a program at Shared Hope that has been both enormous in scale and unparalleled in scope: the Protected Innocence Challenge.

Drew has become a trusted friend and an invaluable resource of expert input over the years. His experience and drive for the fight against child exploitation has been remarkable to watch and his advice is always valued.

In 2012, Shared Hope awarded Drew with a Pathbreaker Award, and not just because he gave us a great idea, but much more for his incredible work in the field of protecting kids. The Pathbreaker is to "recognize the pioneering efforts of individuals throughout the world who broke the trend of inaction and initiated proactive responses to prevent sex trafficking." Drew Oosterbaan most certainly fits that description, and innumerable children have been saved and granted a measure of justice because of his dedication.

12

Identifying Victims to Change Lives

Melissa Snow

"THEY WERE HIDDEN IN PLAIN SIGHT."
MELISSA SNOW

People come into this movement in many ways and for different reasons. They are captured by the stories of victims and survivors, angered by the nature of this horrendous crime, or perhaps they know someone on one of those missing fliers or are just captured by the revelation that sex trafficking exists.

Melissa Snow was captured by the plight of women and girls, and that fed into something much more. With Melissa, I saw a determination I rarely see; she just needed an open door to do something with that drive.

Some people come into this movement for a season and then move on. Others commit their lives to it. Melissa is one of those who has dedicated her life to this moment, and she's made an impact along the way.

It was my pleasure to be part of Melissa's journey.

***

I was sitting in a college class the first time I heard about human trafficking. My professor was telling us how in countries like Uganda, young boys were taken hostage and forced to become child soldiers. As I listened, I suddenly wondered about the girls in these countries. What was happening to them?

I raised my hand and asked, and my professor answered off-handedly, "Oh, the girls are being taken in as concubines to keep fueling more people for the war."

He immediately moved on to something else — but I sat there feeling horrified, imagining these girls taken from their homes and forced into such an awful existence. I couldn't let it go. I had to know more.

After class, I went back to my dorm room and immediately began some research. Terms like *slavery* and *human trafficking* started showing up. Next, I researched to see if there were any groups in the U.S. helping to combat these atrocities. There were larger organizations like UNICEF and UNIFEM talking about this issue, but I wanted something I could focus on locally.

It was in the early 2000s, and there were only a handful of organizations working in the anti-trafficking field. Shared Hope International came up in my search, and I decided to reach out to them, as well as a few others. Though I was just a lowly college student, I couldn't let this go and asked if there was anything I could do to help raise awareness.

Shared Hope sent me some helpful resources, and I utilized them to host some awareness events on campus. I talked to anyone who would listen.

And I soon learned this was an unknown issue to everyone.

About a year and a half later, in 2002, I graduated and moved back to Washington, D.C. One thing was clear: I wanted to continue in this type of work, and I felt bound and determined to somehow work for Shared Hope.

I met with Linda Smith in D.C. and gave her my resume. I tried expressing how passionate I was about being part of the anti-trafficking movement. I was a bright-eyed, bushy-tailed recent graduate with no real experience other than hosting some awareness events and volunteering at programs for homeless youth and victims of sexual assault, but I hoped my passion would make up for whatever else I was lacking.

Linda thanked me and said she was sorry — they didn't have an office in D.C. I was disappointed, but still determined.

"I'll continue doing awareness. This is my passion. I know this is what I was made to do," I told her.

A month later, I got a phone call from Shared Hope. They had received a grant on behalf of the U.S. Department of State to address trafficking in several countries overseas, and Linda had decided it made sense to expand Shared Hope by opening an office in the nation's capital. They offered me an opportunity to apply for an internship, so I did. It was a humble start: I worked in the office with one other woman and did everything from making coffee and putting together Ikea furniture to planning conferences. I was like a sponge — absorbing every moment of shared knowledge and saying yes to every task and project I could. This began eight years with Shared Hope, and my first immersion into the world of trafficking of women and children internationally ... and then right here at home. Like most anti-trafficking organizations in 2002, Shared Hope was mostly focused on combating traffic overseas. With the grant from the Department of State, we were tasked with conducting outreach in several countries and working with government, law enforcement, and local non-organizations to raise awareness about trafficking. Our efforts focused on identifying and lifting up great leaders and doing crucial work in these locations. We recognized our time there was limited, and that these leaders would be the ones left to carry the work forward. Our funding helped coordinate training conferences and develop action plans for addressing trafficking in their communities.

I appreciated Linda's heart in lifting up local leaders rather than trying to plant the Shared Hope flag in each location. Too often in international work, I noticed outside organizations coming in and thinking they knew how to "fix" an issue better than the local community. I saw it as arrogant and culturally insensitive. But Shared Hope was different.

Our work overseas was incredibly successful, and it allowed us to continue to invest in the support of local efforts to provide long-term restoration of women and children. We partnered with organizations to help them develop or expand their services — called Homes of Hope. My absolute favorite moments with Shared Hope came through traveling around to the Homes of Hope in India, Nepal, Fiji, and Jamaica. We would spend days sitting with the survivors and program staff, listening to their stories, successes, hopes, and challenges. I remember so clearly one morning waking up at Ashagram (Home of Hope) in India. I woke up to the sound of rain falling lightly and the beautiful sound of a woman singing. Her voice was joined by another, and then another, until the entire courtyard was filled with joyful singing. I felt so honored to experience that moment. To witness what real healing and recovery looks and feels like and the incredible resiliency of the human spirit.

Another area of effort I appreciated at Shared Hope was the focus to really understand how trafficking happened in a community. We looked at getting to the root causes of this issue and then worked to invest in the local community to help make lasting changes. This mentality — of getting to the heart of communities and their specific economic, cultural, and historical contexts — also helped when we looked at our own country and its regions and communities.

While working internationally, we kept seeing a pattern. While there were foreign national victims being brought in and exploited within communities, there was also a huge population of local women and children being exploited alongside the foreign national population. The fact is, trafficking is all about the money, and it was easier and more cost-effective for traffickers to target people in their own communities instead of bringing in people from other countries.

As we worked in these international settings and found these patterns, we started to look inward at the United States, wondering, "Are there American women and children being exploited in the

U.S., within our own communities?"

We kept asking this question, and looking for the answer. We reached out to survivor-led organizations that were working with other survivors of the commercial sex industry and asked what they were seeing. They shared stories that completely mirrored the exploitation pattern we found with foreign national survivors: traffickers were taking advantage of those who were vulnerable and offering them hope and dreams, then exploiting them for their own profit.

I'll never forget one of the first domestic-trafficking victims I met — during street outreach in Las Vegas. She was eleven years old. Her mother struggled with drug addiction and homelessness. Her first introduction into trafficking was a man who offered her food and lured her into his van. She recalled not having eaten for days and was starving. Once in his van, he told her "nothing in life is free" and proceeded to rape her. Afterward, he gave her a sandwich. He then told her they made a great team.

He sold her for months. She got sandwiches, he kept the money. Despite the sadness in her eyes when I met her, she spoke with incredible strength and optimism in talking about her life goals. We connected her with resources and got her a safe place to stay for the evening. But it didn't feel like enough. I was so angry this little girl's hunger had been preyed upon and exploited.

I stayed connected with her for a few months and was surprised to hear the insane systems and cycles she was forced to navigate at her young age. She bounced from homeless shelters to CPS to always being placed back with her mother. Still homeless, she was left to fend for herself. The last I heard, one of the street outreach workers saw her climbing into the cab of a 16-wheeler truck. They never saw her again. Systems failed her, as she was never reported missing and no one searched for her other than the street outreach team. These children fall through the cracks of our systems every day and are invisible to everyone other than traffickers — the ones who see this supply of vulnerable children as the perfect prey.

Linda, with her background as a Congresswoman, held hearings on the Hill to elevate the issue. We finally got the attention of the Department of Justice — they provided Shared Hope with a grant in 2006 to align with the ten newly funded, human-trafficking task forces.

We were tasked with developing a research tool to conduct assessment of ten U.S. locations to see whether the trafficking of American children in the United States was happening in our country.

I remember a colleague at Shared Hope, Samantha Vardaman, and I were sitting in a hotel room in Houston. We were putting together a methodology on how to do assessments within these local communities to figure out what was happening. We wanted to really look beneath the surface and needed to develop a model to conduct hundreds and hundreds of interviews with professionals who were coming into contact with young people at-risk for trafficking. We were trying to get people to see and share information on a hidden population. We could only do that by obtaining the right information that came from targeting the right people and asking the right questions.

One major problem we discovered was the children being exploited through commercial sex were being misidentified as homeless youth or sexual abuse victims or child prostitutes. By misidentifying them, no one had an accurate understanding of how many children were in trafficking situations or how best to help them. It also allowed communities to say "No, it's not happening here," and look the other way.

When we counted all of the kids identified under these varied labels, the numbers were stunning. Everywhere we looked, we found trafficking victims — not people brought in from other countries, but local kids being commercially, sexually exploited. The traffickers were strangers, parents, boyfriends, coaches ...

Just as frightening was the revelation that because countless children weren't recognized as victims of sex trafficking, they weren't provided the help and services they needed.

We couldn't change anything until we gave these kids an identification with which people would *see* them. Only when they were clearly identified could we get them the help they needed. But how could we begin to change how the entire world thought and talked about these kids? How did we make them visible? They were hidden in plain sight.

Identifying the Victims by Giving Them a Name

This was a major problem in helping trafficking victims. It was a very basic one — an essential one. We couldn't change anything until we had a foundational ability to identify who and what we were talking about.

When people heard about sex trafficking in the United States, they were shocked, but many thought of it as women and girls from other countries smuggled into the U.S. and exploited in prostitution or domestic work.

The research was revealing this wasn't the whole story.

The children who were actually the majority of U.S. victims of trafficking were being misidentified as child prostitutes. They were picked up by police and arrested — charged for the crime being committed against them — or they were dismissed by the systems set up to help abused and exploited youth, such as child welfare and sexual assault programs.

So that first step had to be very basic — we needed a common language.

We needed to create a term that would capture who we were talking about and what they were experiencing.

If we approached judges, law enforcement, child welfare, or juvenile justice — all professional populations that had the potential of coming into contact with these victims — and asked, "Have you identified or have you recovered any American child sex-trafficking victims?" they would have looked at us like we were crazy. It just wasn't a recognized or known entity at that time.

So, sitting in that hotel room in Houston with Samantha, we tried to think through the best way to identify them. We couldn't ask people about *child prostitutes* even if that's how people labeled them. If we continued to use that label, the kids would continue to be stigmatized and blamed, viewed as delinquents when they were the victims. That wouldn't help them at all.

We decided to align the term with the federal Trafficking Victims Protection Act. It clearly defined sex trafficking of a minor in the United States as a person under the age of 18 who is being commercially, sexually exploited.

After a lot of discussion and scribbling down ideas, we came up with the term: Domestic Minor Sex Trafficking, or DMST.

Domestic

We wanted people to realize that we were talking about domestic victims — U.S. citizens and lawful permanent residents.

Minor

We were talking about specifically minors — kids.

Sex Trafficking

According to TVPA, any person under the age of 18 exploited through a commercial sex act is a victim of sex trafficking. It's that simple. Children cannot consent to being rented by the minute — this is sex trafficking.

Identifying the Victims by Seeing Them

Ernie Allen's quote about the only way to not find child sex trafficking in a city was because they just weren't looking was absolutely true. The published project was called the *National Report on Domestic Minor Sex Trafficking*. We discovered that domestic minor sex trafficking was happening in every single location we looked at. By adjusting the lens and creating a shared language, we instigated a paradigm shift that allowed child-serving professionals to see these children and the exploitation they were experiencing.

As we introduced the new DMST name along with the TVPA law, professionals became concerned and wanted to be a part of the solution. They really wanted to know the red flags, what to ask, and how to ask in a way that didn't cause more trauma or communicate bias or blame.

After the problem of giving it a name, one of the biggest factors to undertake was that kids were failing to be identified because of a huge misunderstanding of what trafficking looked like. These children weren't locked away in some underground warehouse. Many were actually right in front of us. They were touching our systems every day: child protective services, juvenile justice, law enforcement, victim advocacy, and direct-serve groups.

The problem was that these services didn't identify them correctly, and, because of that, they were often labeled inappropriately and diverted away from the services they both needed and deserved. And when they did receive services, they were not specific to their exploitation. Service providers didn't understand the complex trauma they had experienced — the trauma bonds holding them psychologically captive to their abuser and the incredibly long road to recovery that lies ahead.

As awareness grew, many professionals were very concerned about the fact that they had interacted with kids and failed them. People needed a resource tool to help with training on identification and response.

At Shared Hope, we felt the responsibility was on us. We were the ones who'd discovered from different survivors and professionals how this crime was operating in so many areas.

I brought an idea of developing a resource to Linda and Samantha, and they blessed it by creating a working group. We knew this task was of critical importance and needed to rely on a team to get it right. We convened a multi-disciplinary team of trauma experts and child experts, child psychologists, survivors, community-based providers that were working with young people, and sat down to develop a resource we could put into the hands of people who had the potential to identify and help these kids.

The multi-part resource package we developed is called *INTERVENE: Identifying and Responding to America's Trafficking Youth.* There's a practitioner's guide that provides an in-depth understanding of the specific dynamics and trauma related to DMST. Next, we developed an intake tool, and then a training video.

The two-tiered intake tool provides professionals working with youth a trauma-informed and strength-based way to collect the red flag indicators on the youth they serve. If those indicators showed potential trafficking, then we provided an additional set of questions that were a bit more direct, helping to unpack some of the at-risk components going on in a child's life. The focus is not on a disclosure but rather collecting the puzzle pieces to bring clearly into view both risk factors and strengths.

The questions were intended to be informal, and a version of one question might look like this:

"It's really tough out there surviving on the streets ... can you tell me how you took care of yourself while you were out?"

Or, "Can you tell me about some of the things that you did to survive?"

This put it in context of survival, on the strength-based perspective that focused on recognizing the skills. By doing that, we took away blame and judgment. We were acknowledging the strength and the skills these kids leveraged to stay alive.

The first tier was an initial screening to collect the indicators and the flags, and second tier went to somebody with more training who was able to identify and appropriately respond to what these kids have been through.

We took our resource and did tons and tons of training with a variety of different service providers and professionals to equip them with this model. The feedback was incredible, and it felt great to provide such a tangible resource to professionals who were eager to help.

When I left Shared Hope to join a Baltimore-based nonprofit to start up their anti-trafficking program, I asked Shared Hope's permission to continue implementing the *Intervene* model. They said not only would they give me permission, but they would fund my implementation of it.

I was getting calls with these incredible stories by CPS workers, juvenile justice, and law enforcement about the training and also asking specific questions that I was incorporating into the training. I wanted to create a partnership to do a pilot version of *Intervene*. So, I wrote a grant to Shared Hope about a pilot using the *Intervene* resource model at a juvenile detention facility.

I found a partnership with an all-girls juvenile detention center in Maryland and sat down with their amazing team. They didn't believe that they had trafficking victims coming through their facility, but they were willing to have the conversation. They essentially said, "We might be missing something, so we're willing to pilot this and figure out how to make it work. Then we'll see what comes from it."

Since *Intervene* is not a static model, we sat down with the team at the detention facility and talked about how to fold the flagging tool into their initial intake process with the kids. We set up a whole process and trained staff on what we were looking for and what questions to ask. We then created a process for flagging the potential high-risk kids. The staff would collect tools throughout a week. I would come into the facility and read over the tools.

After that, one of my coworkers or I would come to the facility weekly to meet with each of these young people who were flagged and have a follow-up conversation with them.

The result was truly one of the most eye-opening processes ever. Within the first two weeks of implementing this process, we identified the first survivor who was already in the facility. And the numbers just kept increasing. These were all kids who were coming in on curfew violations and runaway warrants, sometimes assault, car-theft, or drugs charges. It really ran the gamut.

Through the program, we discovered that many of them also had historical trafficking that had happened, or they were actively being recruited by traffickers, or they were right squarely in the middle of a trafficking incident.

Shared Hope was beside us, supporting us and celebrating the success every step of the way.

We also developed response protocols that included Maryland State Police, FBI Child Exploitation Task Force, Child Protective Services, and the Baltimore Child Advocacy Center. We wanted to make sure when identification and disclosure did occur we had an informed and sensitized team responding.

This was really eye-opening for the juvenile detention staff. They became advocates for the kids and started demanding youth be transferred out of detention and into a more therapeutic setting. In other words, *If this kid is in our detention facility and yes, she stole a car, or yes, she was arrested for drugs, the Trafficking Victims Protection Act says that children should not be held accountable for the crimes committed during the course of their victimization.* They became advocates and realized that these children didn't belong there. If they were holding drugs for their pimp, or their pimp gave them these drugs, or their pimp told them to drive the stolen car, they were traffic victims in these situations. The staff's response was, "This isn't okay, and not on our watch."

It turned into one of the most successful projects I worked on while at the Baltimore-based nonprofit organization for identifying trafficked youth. I'm sure it's evolved over the years, but my understanding is that that program continues today.

The success also gave Shared Hope tangible results for how *Intervene* was working, and how we had adapted it to fit this specific project. We were all thrilled at how these kids' lives were being changed. Since 2010, in even just this one Maryland-based juvenile detention center, children's lives have been completely rerouted because of the program. It's these successes that keep me and all of us in the anti-trafficking movement going and fighting on.

As I look back over the last fifteen years, I'm so grateful I picked up the phone and connected with Shared Hope. I found my calling and my passion, and I've never looked back. I feel honored to do this work, and I've learned so much. I've heard thousands of stories and seen the worst of humanity. I've sat in brothels in India, assisted victims recovered in law enforcement operations around the world and in the U.S., and walked countless hours conducting street outreach in cities across America. But I've also seen significant changes, better laws, great improvements in how kids are treated and helped, and many, many survivors who have turned their tragedy into triumph — I've celebrated countless graduations, birthdays, births, weddings, redeemed relationships, and endless bravery and strength. My life is better, I'm a better person, because of the honor of walking beside these extraordinary survivors. Each of them has greatly impacted and shaped my life.

We continue to face huge problems. Demand is the biggest one. We need to figure out what is causing men (mostly men, but some women too) to do this in the first place. What makes men want to buy sex with kids? And why are men who buy children to rape not being held accountable? That's what we need to know — and figure out how to effect change. The reality is, sex trafficking is a financially motivated crime — for pimps it's all about the money. So demand matters. If there was not a buyer, there would not be a job opportunity for a trafficker to target and exploit vulnerable children. We must get to the root of the issue, because if we're constantly reacting, we will never get ahead of it. If we're constantly reacting instead of dealing with the root, it means another child has been exploited and a life forever impacted. Those who BUY and SELL children must be held accountable.

I'm grateful for my Shared Hope family. I have learned that surrounding myself with the support and love of other fierce advocates makes it possible to get up each day and wage war on those who exploit our children. We cannot do this alone. I won't stop until we've won and ALL children are safe.

IDENTIFYING VICTIMS TO CHANGE LIVES

13

WHO BUYS A CHILD FOR SEX?

DEMAND

WITHOUT BUYERS, THERE WOULD BE NO COMMERCIAL SEX-TRAFFICKING INDUSTRY.

Ten or more men a day. These are the common numbers we've heard again and again by young women who have escaped sex trafficking.

Who are these men paying to have sex with children who are too young to drive, often too young for high school, or too young to enter a PG-13 movie?

The question of who buys traffic victims is one that haunts each one of us fighting to stop the sex trafficking of minors. From my experience, the typical age of entry of girls being sold for sex is middle school — from about eleven to fourteen years old. Many are much younger children.

Without buyers, there would be no commercial sex-trafficking industry.

Children and teenagers would not be lured, manipulated, violated, and their lives destroyed through this heinous victimization. It's an industry fueled by lust and money.

I was awakened to the problem in the United States in 2007. Shared Hope's DEMAND Report revealed staggering numbers. As I worked internationally, I was continually repulsed and angered by the sheer volume of men who sought sex with children forced into prostitution. Girls were taken from villages or sold by their own parents because more product was needed to meet a demand.

As a proud American, I believed we were more civilized, that our kids were more protected than other places in the world. I thought the United States of America was different. I was wrong.

We began to really look at the issue of demand. Who are these people buying American kids for sex?

Who are ALL of these men buying American kids for sex?

While I wanted to envision deranged characters, that scary guy is not the typical profile. Here's what we've found[1]:

- They are mostly men (not surprisingly 99%).
- Most are married and have children of their own.
- They usually have an average to high IQ.
- Many are college-educated (47% arrested in the sting operation *National John's Day*).
- Age range is 18 to 89 years old; average age 42.5 years old.
- 85% prefer female, 15% male.
- Found in every profession, every social class, and in all areas

of society. They are doctors, attorneys, professional athletes, CEOs, ministers, and the dad next door.

- Often, they began by watching porn.
- They don't look or act like bad guys. Many times, no one would guess what they are doing until arrested or perhaps a wife discovers the truth.
- Some view women as objects, but some cherish the women in their lives, just not the ones they buy.
- A "buyer" may be the guy everyone likes, and he's good at keeping his dark secret. That secret often includes sexual addiction that started with viewing porn and escalated to hardcore porn, child porn, and the buying of sex acts with children.
- They are humans who have lost something inside, who struggle with intimacy, and who find sex to be an act of pleasure and not of love.

Some even more specific examples have been revealed through sting operations and prosecutions. A sample of some of the convicted men gives us insights into the people buying or attempting to buy children for sex.

Buyers are individuals who pay for or trade something of value for a sexual act. Also, called "John" or "Trick."

Douglas Hunt was a 52-year-old elementary teacher in West Virginia when he was arrested.[2] He later pled guilty of sexual enticement of a minor. Hunt responded to an internet ad and offered to pay $200 to have sexual interactions with two girls, ages 12 and 13. The ad was posted by an undercover detective. When Hunt arrived at the hotel where the young girls were supposedly waiting, he was arrested.

Hunt was sentenced to 120 *months* in prison and 10 years of supervised release. He was required to surrender all teaching licenses that he held in any state.

Active duty naval recruiter, Shane Childers, age 32, was wearing his Navy uniform, but had taken off his uniform shirt and was wearing a white undershirt, when he knocked on the door of the undercover residence. Childers paid an undercover law enforcement officer $60 to have sex with an 11-year-old girl. He also paid an extra $20 to have intercourse without using a condom.[3]

Childers responded to an online ad using a government-owned computer at the Armed Forces Recruiting Station in Lenexa, Kansas, his Navy email address, and his government-issued cell phone to arrange the transaction.

Childers was sentenced to 15 years in federal prison without parole. The court also ordered Childers to forfeit to the government his 2002 Chrysler Sebring, which he used to commit the offense.

In February 2011, state and federal law enforcement officers worked undercover in Sioux Falls, South Dakota. They placed several online advertisements in their attempts to apprehend people seeking children for sex. Officers pretended to be a man offering his girlfriend's minor daughters for sex while his girlfriend was out of town.

One man who responded to the advertisement was Daron Lee Jungers. After several e-mails discussing details about the girls, their ages, prices, and after receiving an age-regressed photograph of adult female officers, Jungers indicated that he wanted an eleven-year-old girl for an hour so that she could perform oral sex on him.

Jungers traveled from Sioux City, Iowa, to the house in Sioux Falls where law enforcement officers had set up the undercover operation. Jungers confirmed he would pay for oral sex from the eleven-year-old, but he was uncomfortable doing so at the house and asked to take the girl with him instead. Police arrested Jungers when he entered the house.

Ronald Bonestroo agreed to meet an undercover agent at the house after several emails and recorded telephone conversations about the girls and the rates for sex with them. After receiving an age-regressed photograph, Bonestroo agreed to pay $200 to have sex with the fourteen-year-old twin girls for an hour. When Bonestroo arrived at the house, he asked if the twins were there and showed the undercover officer the money he brought to complete the transaction. Officers arrested Bonestroo shortly thereafter.[4]

The sentencing of Jungers and Bonestroo would prove especially challenging when a judge initially dismissed the jury's guilty conviction. Another judge eventually overturned this judge's ruling and let the jury's guilty verdict stand, but it demonstrated the ongoing challenges of convictions in child-trafficking cases.

> The market is driven by these men. Buyers create and flourish a market that enslaves and victimizes American children again and again.

In March 2012, Marcelo Alejo Desautu was sentenced to seventeen years in prison and ten years supervised release for sex trafficking of a minor.

Desautu, 39, was caring for a twelve-year-old girl when he gave her drugs and alcohol and then sold her for sex to adult men. Desautu used the money to buy drugs for himself, and he also had sex with the girl.

"This defendant earned a substantial sentence in federal prison when he drugged and sexually exploited a twelve-year-old girl, forever altering the course of her life," said U.S. Attorney Yates about the case. "It is unfathomable that there is even a market for the sale of such a young child for sex. This lengthy sentence should deter others who would consider engaging in similar heinous acts."

One of the men who paid Desautu to have sex with the twelve-year-old was a businessman, Peter Privateer. He pled guilty to the crime.

This case was part of Project Safe Childhood. It was investigated by the Cobb County Police Department and the FBI.[5]

Then there are the most heinous stories ...

While these are all deplorable, some go into realms of evil that the average person could not conjure in their darkest imagining. But the fact

Shared Hope's Demanding Justice Report 2014 studied 134 cases of buyers in child sexual exploitation cases — the target cities: Seattle, Phoenix, Portland, DC–Baltimore Corridor. Of these 134 cases:

- 15 went free
- 119 arrests
- One was dropped
- 118 prosecuted
- 5 dismissed
- 107 pled guilty
- 6 went to trial
- None were acquitted
- 113 guilty verdicts
- 26% served no time
- 69% of guilty had sentences suspended

is, there are not just evil people in the world — these people have connected and are networking with one another and often ahead of law enforcement efforts by decades.

In 2011, Australian citizen Peter Truong and his American partner Mark Newton were arrested and convicted as sex offenders. In 2005, the couple bought a Russian baby for $8,000 and falsified documents to appear that the baby was their son. Within weeks of getting the newborn, the men began sexually abusing him, filming, and sharing the videos with an international pedophilia group, an online group that had remained hidden for twenty years. As the boy grew, they began to travel the world selling the child for sex to at least eight members of this group.

> Bonestroo was convicted and never contested his crime of paying for sex with a child. However, during the initial overturning of the jury's conviction, the court held that "no reasonable jury could have found Bonestroo guilty of that offense beyond a reasonable doubt, and his conviction must be overturned."
>
> Bonestroo's acquittal was overturned by the Eighth Circuit Opinion, and his conviction of attempted commercial sex trafficking of a minor reinstated.

Peter Truong was convicted and received a thirty-year sentence, reduced due to cooperation in locating the other men who abused the child.

His partner was convicted with a forty-year sentence.

Two of the other abusers included an American junior tennis coach and an American attorney in Florida.

The young boy was placed with extended family in the United States.

[1] Shared Hope International. "Demanding Justice Report" (pps. 50-55). https://sharedhope.org/wp-content/uploads/2014/08/Demanding_Justice_Report_2014.pdf, 2014.

[2] Former West Virginia Elementary Teacher Sentenced 120 Months for Sexual Enticement of a Minor. archives.FBI.gov, Accessed September 14, 2018.

[3] Whitworth, Matt J. "News Release: Human Trafficking Rescue Project." Justice.gov, October 19, 2009.

[4] *United States* v. Junger. http://caselaw.findlaw.com/us-8th-circuit/1620002.html.

[5] "Georgia Man Sentenced to 17 Years in Prison for Sex Trafficking of a Minor." The United States Department of Justice. https://www.justice.gov/opa/pr/georgia-man-sentenced-17-years-prison-sex-trafficking-minor, March. 21, 2012.

14

THE BATTLE FOR OUR CHILDREN'S MINDS

EXPOSING CHILDREN TO PORN EARLY IN LIFE DESENSITIZES AND LURES THEM, ENSURING FUTURE PROFIT FROM ADDICTION.

Logan was sitting on the couch in his Taekwondo uniform playing a game on his mom's phone while he waited for them to leave. His mom, Lisa, had been a stay-at-home mom who'd recently gone back to school part-time since both of her kids had crossed into the double-digit ages of ten and twelve. Lisa was careful about Logan being on the Internet and hadn't gotten him his own phone yet, but there were a couple of online kid games she allowed on her phone for him to play.

Logan opened an app and began tapping the screen. He scrolled furiously and tapped some more.

"Yes!" he shouted. "Level eight!"

A new yellow icon appeared in the corner, flashing and twirling. He recognized the image as a popular kids' character. *Maybe this was a new game his mom would let him get.*

He touched the icon and the phone screen showed a new image. Logan stared for a long moment, trying to figure out what he was looking at.

"Ew! Mom! That's disgusting. Mom!"

Lisa came out of the bathroom where she had been putting on her earrings.

"What is it?"

"There's a naked woman on your phone! I just touched one button and it came up."

Lisa froze a moment, then rushed over and grabbed the phone. She put her hand over mouth when she saw the advertisement for nude pictures and free online chatting.

"How did you get on this?" she demanded, but then she immediately realized that if her son weren't telling the truth, he would have never called her.

"I thought it was a kid's game, I promise!" Logan was close to tears.

Lisa hugged her son and felt sick to her stomach. The image wasn't just of a naked woman, but a very seductive and sexual pose. In one moment, her son was exposed to something she'd worked hard to protect him from, and in their own house.

This was exactly how pubescent boys could get drawn into pornography. She couldn't take back the image he'd seen. Lisa also knew that next time such an image might not create such a horrified reaction from her son.

***

Every day, stories like this play out in today's online culture. As the next generation of boys grow into adulthood, experts are becoming increasingly concerned about the different aspects of technology and what's available through it — and how it is affecting brain development.

If you've ever handed a smartphone to a busy toddler, you know today's devices are designed to be instinctive. A child can navigate screens as easily as pushing around blocks. With a phone, a child cannot only delete emails, make phone calls, and send texts filled with emojis, they can also watch videos.

Drawn to video images, a child will eventually find dangerous sites and click until he finds something that catches his attention. This is not an accident.

Popular video, social media, online media sites, and others can be dangerous places for children. Even though many sites have strict terms of use prohibiting pornography and graphic content, countless popular internet companies have been accused of doing little to monitor or restrict inappropriate content. Many innocent search terms will bring up hardcore, violently explicit videos because uploaders use misleading descriptions when adding the content. This leaves kids wide open to exposure to porn.

The porn industry banks on the ability of children to navigate and utilize technology for entertainment. These big-business sex brokers make it simple for adults to find porn images, but the fact that children can also search and see what they're selling is a bonus. Exposing children to porn early in life desensitizes and lures them, ensuring future profit from addiction.

According to Dr. Jennifer Brown, pornography affects the developing brain of the child in more ways than one. When a child is exposed to sexually explicit material, it causes the child's body to release stress hormones, also known as the "fight or flight" response. These hormones trigger an instant, involuntary, and lasting biochemical trail. In other words, emotionally and sexually arousing images imprint and alter the child's brain.

Neurotransmitters (dopamine and norepinephrine) and hormones (cortisol, norepinephrine, and testosterone) have been called the "stress compounds." These compounds inhibit the prefrontal cortex and activate the amygdala, stimulating the basal ganglia. The prefrontal cortex of a child's brain directs things such as self-control, emotional regulation, analysis, and complex cognitive behavior. The amygdala releases neurotransmitters that stimulate the basal ganglia. The basal ganglia, when stimulated, causes a child to become compulsive, creates a loss of natural empathy and sympathy for others, and makes a child much more likely to engage in addictive behaviors. The child becomes more impulsive and driven by immediate gratification.[1]

In other words, children are becoming early addicts. Sounds like the perfect target market for porn producers, doesn't it?

In addition to a flood of stress hormones, the hypothalamus also activates the testes to secrete testosterone. Children exposed repeatedly to sexually explicit material find themselves entering puberty with a ramped-up sex drive and few tools to control behavior. These boys and girls grow into adults, and bring their addictions with them into relationships.

Psychology Today published the results of an online survey of more than 4,000 people in 2014. They found that individuals wishing to stop their pornography viewing are having a difficult time doing so. Their frequency of viewing pornography (three to five times a week or more) is related to elevated depression, anxiety, and loneliness.

Over time, some men find that viewing porn no longer satisfies them. Dr. Victor B. Cline, a clinical psychologist and psychotherapist specializing in marital and family counseling and the treatment of sexual compulsions and addictions, has said it this way:

> With the passage of time, the addicted person required rougher, more explicit, more deviant and 'kinky' kinds of sexual material to get their "highs" and "sexual turn-ons." It was reminiscent of individuals afflicted with drug addictions. Over time there is nearly always an increasing need

Fifty years ago, pornography was seen as entertainment provided by willing adult actors; but today, images of child sexual exploitation represent a perverted new frontier. Early warriors saw that viewing pornographic magazines and videos that could be purchased in "adult" bookstores led to the consumers' desire to act out what they viewed, going to the streets to access women in prostitution. Those early in the fight made great headway in closing down outlets of pornography, and, in fact, in the 1980s the FBI declared that pornography was under control. Then came the birth of the internet, which enabled proliferation of adult pornography and met the ever-increasing desire for images of younger and younger children being sexually violated. Today we know that images of child sexual exploitation are images of a sex-trafficked child. One of the early warriors against pornography in all its forms was Patrick Truman, whose organization, the National Center on Sexual Exploitation, is one of the strongest voices calling the growing menace of pornography a worldwide public health problem.

At Shared Hope International, we have seen the tie between trafficking and pornography many times. In one case, a male survivor of the heinous act of familial trafficking was sold for sex by his own father. Some of his early memories include his father taking pictures of him and other children forced into uncomfortable behaviors that he didn't understand at the time. Looking back, he believes these images were likely shared with other predators.

for more of the stimulant to get the same initial effect. Being married or in a relationship with a willing sexual partner did not solve their problem. Their addiction and escalation were mainly due to the powerful sexual imagery in their minds, implanted there by the exposure to pornography.[2]

Relational and emotional security isn't the only thing affected by porn addiction. Porn-addicted men are more likely to suffer from erectile dysfunction and are less likely to be satisfied with sexual intercourse, according to survey findings presented at the American Urological Association's annual meeting in Boston in May of 2017. And those men studied weren't middle-aged. In fact, some of them were as young as twenty.

According to a study published on the site for the U.S. National Library of Medicine, there has been a sharp rise in erectile dysfunction, delayed ejaculation, decreased sexual satisfaction, and diminished libido during partnered sex in men under forty. And this trend isn't just American men. There are studies around the world that are pointing to the same conclusion: **porn-induced sexual dysfunction is on the rise.**[3]

You would think that fact alone would have men turning off their computers, but the addiction is real.

The progression looks like this:

- An adolescent boy accidentally comes across a porn site. He's curious and sees what he's never known about before. *So, this is what everyone means when they joke around or talk about sex.*

- The boy's friends may look with him or talk about the online things they experience. The accessibility is easy, and they quickly share ways to hide what they're seeing from their parents.

- The boy continues to view porn sites, and culture says this is natural and part of growing up.

- He becomes desensitized to what he's already seen again and again and becomes intrigued with the hard-core and explicit porn sites, which are also easy to access.

- The boy has his own sexual experiences, but they don't reflect the sexual experiences he's accustomed to seeing online.

- The boy is less satisfied with the hard-core sites and needs more to find satisfaction. He's already been to live chats and viewed live sexual acts.

- The boy sees an ad online advertising commercial sex. After a first time of paying for sex, he finds it more gratifying than what he experiences with girlfriends and eventually his wife.

- The boy sees ads for younger girls, and the images excited him as he hasn't been excited in some time.

- The boy is a man convicted of child sex trafficking offenses, sentenced to years in prison, and will be a registered sex offender for the remainder of his life.

Today, the Internet is a useful tool for predators to get their target.

[1] How Pornography Affects the Brain. Brown, Jennifer. www.slideshare.net, uploaded December 12, 2014.

[2] Cline, Dr. Victor B. "Pornography's Effects on Adults and Children." Catholicenewsagency.com, Accessed September 2018.

[3] Park, Brian Y; Wilson, Gary; Berger, Jonathan; Christman, Matthew; Reina, Bryn; Bishop, Frank; Klam, Warren P.; and Doan, Andrew P. "Is Internet Pornography Causing Sexual Dysfunctions? A Review with Clinical Reports." U.S. National Library of Medicine National Institutes of Health, August 5, 2016.

15

BRIANNA'S CLOSE CALL

"I HAD BEEN CHOSEN."

BRIANNA MYERS

It had been a long week and was nearly Christmas when I met Brianna under harrowing conditions and in a moment when her life could have been destroyed forever. We both would change each other's lives.

Christmas lights glittered on the houses on my street, a reminder that the world does not stop while we fight evil. I looked forward to the coming holidays with my family and to celebrating the birth of Christ. The past few months had been a whirlwind of meetings, interviews, and strategizing with my team. The word was finally spreading about sex trafficking in the United States. People around the country were waking up to the fact that children were being sold right under our noses. It was progress, but it seemed progress was constantly impeded by new revelations or challenges against what we sought to accomplish.

My husband, Vern, had just turned on the engine of our car hoping the heater would warm quickly against the cold December day. Then I got the call.

John, a Lieutenant for the Vancouver Police Department and a strong ally of Shared Hope, was on the other end. I greeted him, then tensed at his tone.

"Hey, Linda. I need your help."

I'd been impressed by how John was connected to his community. We'd first connected in 2009 when he called me out of the blue to ask if we could meet. His team had discovered what looked like trafficking, but he had some questions. We met, and then he attended a SHI training, which gave him a crash-course in domestic minor sex trafficking. He organized a county-wide group to participate in the FBI's Operation Cross Country sting operation. The two 16-year-old young women they recovered were a wake-up call to his department. Those same officers cohosted with Shared Hope a training the following month for the entire department, juvenile justice workers, and others who work with this population of youth. The Vancouver, WA, police and County Sheriff's office became strong allies in the fight against sex trafficking in the Portland/ Vancouver area.

But now as I sat in my car, listening to his story, my blood ran cold. A young girl named Brianna was being lured into trafficking and they were afraid they were going to lose her. Her friend and family members were doing everything they could to get through to her before she hopped on a flight to Arizona. John was

BRIANNA'S CLOSE CALL

convinced that if she went to Arizona, she'd disappear forever.

"She's eighteen, so there's not a lot I can do. But Linda, this is a good kid. She's a senior in high school, has good grades, volunteers in the community, plans to go to college, and has a strong family."

This was surprising to hear. Most of the young women lured into trafficking were often already struggling in difficult situations. That Brianna came from such a stable background spoke to the level of expertise in these traffickers.

"If we can pin her down, will you come talk with her?"

I agreed immediately. No matter how full my schedule was, this was what we were fighting for. I knew our best chance to help Brianna was right then and there. If traffickers took her far away from her family and friends, chances were they'd never get her back.

I gave John my word that if he called, I'd be there. I kept my phone close, waiting for it to ring. I was touring some property later that day as a possible site for a shelter for survivors when my phone buzzed in my pocket.

"Do you have her?" I asked when I heard John's voice on the line.

"We do," he said quickly. "She's at her friend's house, but

Although a trafficker initially uses the promise of love, adventure, and opportunity to lure victims, they eventually use violence, fear, and intimidation to control them. (sharedhope.org/what-is-sex-trafficking)

not for long. Can you come now? I'm afraid she's going to bolt. My wife and I are hosting a Christmas party at my house. I'll send you the address."

I had to fight the impulse to run as I headed for my car. I knew time was of the essence. John had said Brianna had just turned eighteen. They couldn't hold her for her own safety like they could for a juvenile. Even though we knew she was in danger, as a new adult, we couldn't violate her privacy or her right to leave town if she wished. I just hoped I wasn't too late, and I prayed that her heart would soften enough to listen.

When I reached Brianna's friend's house, she was not happy to see me. She can tell that part of the story ...

***

I was pacing, fuming mad. My friend Evan had betrayed me. My parents were here and this whole thing had blown up into a huge mess.

Glancing at the clock, I calculated the few hours to drive to Seattle. I needed to get back there. Nick would be waiting. Was it possible I had only met him a month earlier?

I worked after school in the diner, a place my two sisters had also worked during their senior years of high school. Nick was seated in my section with his college friend. He was tall, blonde, and perfect. He was older than me at age twenty-four, but I felt like I had won the lottery. That afternoon as I waited on them, Nick and his friend made me feel so beautiful, like I was the center of his universe. No one had made me feel the way Nick did. Nick gave me his number, and he told me to call that night. I didn't usually make bold moves, but this time I did.

Nick and I had talked for hours, almost until the sun came up. I did most of the talking. Nick was so interested in me, made me feel important, and treated me both with respect and like an adult. Like me, he was frustrated that my parents wanted me to go to community college and live at home after graduation. I was eighteen now, officially an adult. My family treated me like I was still a kid. Over the next week, Nick and I talked or texted constantly. I could hardly think of anything else.

"Why don't you drive to Seattle for the weekend," he'd asked. I'd dreamed of moving to Seattle, and the fact that he lived there was another piece to what was right with him. We had so much in common.

"I'll introduce you to some of my friends. We can drive around and look at the city, see the sights. We can drive by the nursing school, and I'll help you look for a job. It will be fun!"

I knew I'd need to lie to my parents to go. They would never let me go to Seattle with some guy they didn't know and whom I'd just met. Nick was treating me with total respect, and hadn't even kissed me, but still they wouldn't say yes.

"Okay," I said. "I just have to figure out what to say to my parents."

Nick helped me come up with a cover story and the weekend plans were set into motion. I was so excited. Seattle was my dream. I wanted to go to nursing school, rent a cool apartment, meet new people. This would be a chance to see what my dream was going to look like.

I'd borrowed my dad's car and drove north, my heart beating fast the whole way. As I pulled into the driveway of Nick's house, I gasped. It looked like a mansion. The Victorian house sat on the edge of a lake, and there were luxury cars in the driveway. I looked down at my outfit and wished I had dressed up more.

Nick made me feel so welcome. He introduced me to everyone like he was proud to be my boyfriend. I had never felt that spoiled in my life. For the entire weekend, I was shown a world I'd never known. Some of it made me nervous and pushed the limits of my comfort zone, but everyone treated me like an adult and worked hard to make me feel comfortable in such a grown-up world.

Then Nick offered to take me somewhere warm and sunny for Christmas break. He and a few of his friends were going to Arizona. I had never been to Arizona, and right about now sunshine and a swimming pool sounded like heaven. Because the flight was last minute, he couldn't get me a seat on his flight, but he'd bought me my own ticket. I would leave before him and some of his friends would pick me up from the airport. When I hesitated at the arrangement, he assured me that he'd be just hours behind and I'd be well taken care of. I believed him and could hardly wait. It was all like a dream.

And now that dream was in danger. I had driven my dad's car home and had asked my closest friend Evan to drive me back to Seattle so I could catch my flight. Instead, Evan betrayed me. He told our parents about Nick and refused to drive me back. I needed to call Nick. I needed to get back to him, but my parents, Evan, and his parents were asking me to wait. Evan's dad had called the police. They were treating me like a child, but I wasn't waiting much longer to leave. The problem was that I needed a ride.

I heard a car pull up in the driveway. *Great, a cop*, I thought. I couldn't believe what a big deal everyone was making of this. Kids grew up and went on trips all the time. I just couldn't figure out why

BRIANNA'S CLOSE CALL

everyone was freaking out. *Why wouldn't they let me be an adult and live my own life?* It was time to finally stand up for myself, just like Nick had said.

The door opened, and an attractive, professional woman appeared. She stared at me as she walked in, smiling softly.

My mother said that she knew Linda Smith from the news; she was a former Congresswoman. Linda introduced herself and said she had been called because she was an expert in determining if situations like mine were what the law called trafficking. This was where some smooth guys tricked at times very smart girls like me and put them into prostitution.

Are you kidding me? I thought. *Who's next? Obama?*

I spent the next ten minutes defending myself, acting as grown-up as I knew how. My parents were overreacting, I said. They were overprotective and just didn't want me to leave home. Tensions were high in the house. I was ready to go. If I had to, I could catch a bus or train to Seattle with the clothes on my back and the new cell phone Nick had given me. He had promised to get me a new wardrobe anyway.

"I'll tell you what," said Linda, looking right at me. "Why don't we go for coffee and talk. You tell me what's happening, and I'll tell you what I know. At the end of it, if you still want to go, I'll drive you back to Seattle myself."

There was something about the way Linda carried herself, spoke to me, looked right into my eyes. She wasn't treating me like a child. It was my best option at this point, so I followed her out of that tense house.

Over a cup of coffee, I listened to Linda talk about

trafficking. She told me how guys lured young women by being "perfect," respectful, and someone you'd consider bringing home to meet your parents. But then they'd start isolating a girl, having her not tell her parents and friends much about him — always with some good explanation as to why.

At first, I was completely convinced she was wrong. There was no way Nick had bad intentions. It was awful what Linda was talking about, but that wasn't what was happening here. Then she started saying things that strangely mirrored words Nick had said. She told me what these guys did and said to girls, and they were just what Nick had said and done. She talked about how they might impress with their lavish lifestyles, but they didn't really explain where their money came from. They might work as a team and plot things together.

There had been a few things Nick had said that were so coincidental — and so exact — to what I'd told other guests in the diner, especially one person in particular, that now I wondered if our connection was really as destined as I'd believed. *Had it been plotted?*

It was bizarre listening to Linda throw out things a trafficker might do, and to realize Nick was doing exactly those things to me. Nick and I had fallen head-long hard and fast into a relationship, yet, I didn't know much about his life even after going to Seattle.

When my phone died — my charger had gone missing, which was another ploy Linda talked about — he'd given me "one of his phones" to keep in touch, promising to buy me an iPhone and new clothes after he helped me find a job. He'd lavishly spent money on me.

And then Linda asked me a hard question. "Did he suggest

BRIANNA'S CLOSE CALL

any specific type of job for you in Seattle? Dancing? Stripping?"

I looked down at my coffee. How did she know? I hadn't told a soul about my three days visiting Nick in Seattle. I felt sick. If my parents knew, it would devastate them. I didn't want to tell her; I didn't want anyone to know.

I'd never imagined even going into such a place, but Nick had this way of making me feel like an adult and admired, but for a moment, he and his friends thought I might be too young to go there. I showed them that I wasn't.

"He took me to a place where I could ... dance, if I wanted," I whispered.

"Dance?" she asked.

"Yes," I said, glancing up and biting my lip. "But that's all. It was totally legal. I got my fingerprints and filled out all the papers, just so I wouldn't get in trouble. Nick was always close and told me I didn't have to do anything I didn't want to do. Nick's old girlfriend earned $800 a night dancing and put herself through college. She got

> Trafficking is built on the economic principle of supply and demand. Buyers who are willing to pay for commercial sex acts make the market profitable. Traffickers will seek to capitalize on this market by manipulating and luring victims to meet the demand of buyers.
>
> Commonly, traffickers will build a relationship with a victim in efforts to understand their desires and vulnerabilities and foster emotional attachment. The trafficker may use these desires and vulnerabilities to manipulate the victim, isolate them from friends and family, and use force, violence, threats, and/or intimidation to control the victim. (sharedhope.org)

to pick her own hours and work part-time. I barely make $80 a day at the diner, on a good shift."

"Brianna," Linda leaned over the table, looking me directly in the eyes, and said, "if Nick is a trafficker, you and your family could be in danger. Would one more day make a difference?"

"What?" I shook my head. I couldn't believe it.

"If his intent is not really to send you to Arizona on vacation but for another reason, there's a good chance you won't be back."

It still was too hard to believe, even though other warning signs were now ablaze in my mind. Things I'd overlooked at the time, since, after all, Nick was so good to me.

"Will you at least stay home tonight? Read this little book I wrote that shows you how the traffickers work and decide for yourself. Will it hurt to wait just one more day?"

I nodded, but something in me knew. That night, from Linda's suggestion, we hid my dad's car at the hospital where my mom worked instead of leaving it in the driveway. She told us that Nick and his friends might come looking for me, and if they didn't see the car they wouldn't know I was home.

Looking back now, I know that meeting with Linda saved my life. It seems crazy that I fell for Nick's scheme, but he was that good. Over time, I learned the horrible truth about the danger I was flirting with; I heard the stories of young women who hadn't escaped as I had.

Trafficking was real. It was here in my town, and it happened to me. I thought I was choosing a new life. The truth was, I had been chosen, targeted, and was nearly lured into a life of being forever damaged, if I escaped with my life at all.

BRIANNA'S CLOSE CALL

***

In the days that followed, we learned that Nick was indeed a trafficker. The Victorian mansion Brianna had visited was not his house. The "friends" at the party Nick invited Brianna to attend were actually potential buyers. Brianna's plane ride was a one-way ticket, and Nick had no plans to follow her to Arizona. Brianna had most likely been sold, and she had no idea.

That night, Brianna's dad looked through the curtains and saw a car with its lights off pull into his driveway. It sat for a few minutes before it pulled away; her trafficker seeking to protect his investment.

Looking back, we can see Nick had systematically alienated Brianna from her family. He manipulated her emotions and fed her dreams. We learned that the initial way he did this was through another customer at the diner. For six months before Brianna met

Pimps/traffickers often exhibit the following behaviors or characteristics:

- Jealous, controlling, violent
- Significantly older than female companions
- Promise things that seem too good to be true
- Encourage victims to engage in illegal activities to achieve their goals and dreams
- Buys expensive gifts or owns expensive items
- Is vague about his/her profession
- Pushy or demanding about sex
- Encourages inappropriate sexual behavior
- Makes the victim feel responsible for his/her financial stability; very open about financial matters

Warning signs that an individual is being trafficked:

- Signs of physical abuse like burn marks, bruises, or cuts
- Unexplained absences from class

- Less appropriately dressed than before
- Sexualized behavior
- Overly tired in class
- Withdrawn, depressed, distracted, or checked out
- Brags about making or having lots of money
- Displays expensive clothes, accessories, or shoes
- New tattoo (tattoos are often used by pimps as a way to brand victims — tattoos of a name, symbol of money, or barcode could indicate trafficking)
- Older boyfriend or new friends with a different lifestyle
- Talks about wild parties or invites other students to attend parties
- Shows signs of gang affiliation (i.e. a preference for specific colors, notebook doodles of gang symbols, etc.)

Source: sharedhope.org

Nick, an older gentleman visited the diner and became friends with Brianna. He learned details about her that Nick used later to lure her in. He learned about her dream to move to Seattle, to go to nursing school, to travel. He appeared harmless, like just another friendly customer in the diner.

It seems overwhelming to fight against criminals who are so organized and focused on luring victims.

Brianna's story is a shining example of the impact of education and awareness. Evan's father had attended a training at his local rotary club. He had shared what he knew with his son. When Evan saw the signs that Brianna was being groomed for trafficking, he put things into motion to save his friend.

We are all so thankful for the people who came together to save Brianna. It will take all of us to stop the selling of kids for sex. It will take all of us to make a difference.

Today, Brianna is a nurse and often a spokesperson for Shared Hope. She has become the one responding when police and advocates need to intervene — to have someone listen to a girl on the brink of falling into this horrible slavery. In addition, Brianna's story has impacted thousands through the film and learning materials called *Chosen*.

16

Victims Charged with the Crime that Victimized Them

IF NINA HAD RECEIVED HELP AS A VICTIM INSTEAD OF THAT FIRST CONVICTION, HER ENTIRE LIFE WOULD BE DIFFERENT.

They were victimized by their pimps, by the innumerable buyers who paid for them, and then by the law meant to protect them.

Children should never be arrested for prostitution. No one under the age of eighteen should have a criminal record for the rest of their lives for being trafficked, sold for sex. What they endure is sexual abuse and rape, and every minor should get victim help and services, not a criminal record that limits future opportunities for employment, housing, and education.

This is changing, and it is becoming less frequent, but the fact is, there are still places in our country where an underage girl or boy will be charged with the crimes of prostitution and put into a detention center instead of being offered victim help.

Nina ran away from home at age fourteen. She believed she'd found a safe place when she met a woman who put her up in a hotel room for the night. Instead, the woman forced her into the commercial sex industry.

For the next thirteen years, Nina had twenty different pimps who advertised her for sex on the Internet and abused her verbally and physically. When she was finally referred to victim services, Nina had been convicted of fifty-two offenses, mostly prostitution and related crimes (her first conviction was at age sixteen), and she had spent time in both juvenile hall and jail.

Fourteen-year-old Nina was told by her pimp that if she went to the police for help, she'd get prosecuted as a prostitute. This was exactly what happened. Kids on the street or in these situations rarely seek help from the police. Some don't trust law enforcement. Some have been convinced that they are loved by their pimps, and they feel attached to them and afraid to be apart from them. Whatever their reason, we know it is not a safe or healthy place for a child.

If Nina had received help as a victim instead of that first conviction, her entire life would be different.

Police should be viewed as heroes to these kids out on the streets. Instead, law enforcement is viewed as judgment and criminalization to these young people.

As we have worked to bring together teams of law

Victims Charged with the Crime that Victimized Them

enforcement professionals, politicians, and survivor leaders to create change, one thing has become apparent: victims should not be treated like criminals. This has been a huge part of our driving force behind the training we do with law enforcement around the country.

Had victims like Nina crossed paths with someone who had training in identifying sex trafficking, her path would have looked very different. Instead of being labeled as a "criminal" or "offender" at an early age, Nina could have received the assistance she needed earlier to survive and find restoration for her life.

We know that sex trafficking has devastating consequences on children and adults, including long-lasting physical and psychological trauma, disease (including HIV/AIDS), drug addiction, unwanted pregnancy, malnutrition, social ostracism, and even death.

When survivors later try to rebuild their lives with a heavy criminal record, the odds aren't just against them, it's often impossible for them to recover. How do these kids become adults and live new lives when they are burdened by the damage caused by their traffickers and buyers in addition to the life constraints, burden, social stigma, and personal stigma that come with a criminal record?

In some states, trafficking victims with prosecutions for crimes committed as a result of being subjected to trafficking can have their records expunged or vacated under Vacatur laws.

In the United States, several states are enacting provisions that provide survivors the ability to seek a court order vacating or expunging criminal convictions entered against them that resulted from their trafficking situation. New York led the way to pass a law

> When a child is sold for sex or a person 18 or older has been exploited in commercial sex through means of force, fraud, or coercion, he or she is a victim of sex trafficking, not a perpetrator of a crime.

in 2010, and Florida took it even further when they provided lawful expungement of "any conviction for an offense committed while ... a victim of human trafficking."

Having a criminal record vacated creates legal freedom and redemption. Vacatur is the formal recognition of "factual innocence."

We believe that states should ensure that Vacatur laws include convictions for a wide variety of crimes that victims are forced to commit. All convictions, even misdemeanors, should be vacated.

You can see what a huge development this can be for sex-trafficked victims. These laws, and more like them, not only allow victims to correct past injustices, but also help the children and adults coming out of trafficking situations to reclaim and rebuild their lives. It also reduces the risk of them being "re-trafficked."

When survivors of sex trafficking try to rebuild their lives with a criminal record, they can encounter enormous obstacles. Some rights and lifestyle needs that can be denied after conviction of a crime include the following and vary by states and counties:

- Some jobs deny applicants with criminal records
- No employment in certain fields such as medical and those working with children
- Inapplicable for some public social benefits such as SSI, welfare, public housing, food stamps, and other services (depends on the state and/or county)

VICTIMS CHARGED WITH THE CRIME THAT VICTIMIZED THEM

- Ineligibility for federal financial aid, grants, and student loans
- Loss of parental rights and benefits
- Difficulty renting a home
- Some insurance companies deny felons
- Loss of the right to vote
- Unable to take state bar exams to become an attorney
- Loses right to own a gun
- Loss of right to travel abroad to certain countries
- Cannot serve on a jury
- May lose right to remain in the U.S.

Vacatur laws restore freedoms and rights while helping to correct past injustices. They offer help to trafficking victims in reclaiming and rebuilding their lives, which in turn increases a survivor's chance of finding work and otherwise reducing economic vulnerabilities that can create the risk of being re-trafficked as a means of survival.

In the absence of Vacatur laws, trafficking victims are condemned to a lifetime of hindered rights and economic constraint. They also have a higher chance of future criminal activity if they've only experienced the dark underbelly of America since the time they were first trafficked.

Added to that is also the personal, mental, and spiritual toll. The self-worth and self-image of women and men with a past of being trafficked is already severely damaged. When they wear the label of *criminal*, they are perpetually viewed as former criminals, and even worse, they may view themselves in this way. Restoration then becomes severely handicapped.

Without expunging or vacating, criminal records last a lifetime.

17

A Survivor's Story

SARAH'S YOUNGEST DAUGHTER, CHLOE, ASKED HER WEEKLY IF SHE'D HELP IN HER CLASSROOM LIKE THE OTHER MOMS. SARAH DIDN'T KNOW HOW TO EXPLAIN TO HER DAUGHTERS THAT AS A CRIMINAL AND REGISTERED SEX OFFENDER, SHE COULDN'T. HER PAST HAUNTED (AND STILL DOES) SO MANY AREAS OF HER LIFE.

This survivor's story is fictionalized from true events.

On Sarah's thirty-fourth birthday, her two young girls gave her a birthday party with homemade decorations and a chocolate birthday cake they made with Mom's help. Millie and Chloe would not let their mom help decorate the cake, though, or even see the process. Sarah had to hold back a laugh when she saw the finished product. The cake was roughly covered in chocolate frosting, as was a good portion of the table, and there were enough sprinkles to make every bite crunchy.

It was a good birthday for Sarah; one of the best she'd had.

She and her girls played a card game that Sarah had enjoyed when she was young. The birthday milestone made Sarah think of her journey to experience such a simple and enjoyable day.

As she tucked her girls into bed on a single mattress on the floor of their one-bedroom apartment, Sarah's oldest daughter, Millie, brought up wanting a cell phone for her birthday. Though only in third grade, some of Millie's friends at school had phones. Sarah wanted to blurt out that this wasn't going to happen until Millie was eighteen.

The truth was, Sarah couldn't afford the phone, and she was protective of her girls — maybe more than protective. Sarah regularly battled insomnia brought on by her intense fear and paranoia that something might happen to her daughters. As a survivor of child sex trafficking, Sarah endured evils she hoped her girls would not know existed in the world, let alone experience.

As a child, Sarah's uncle volunteered to care for her after school and on weekends while her mother worked or went out with one of her boyfriends. His hugs and requests for her to sit on his lap soon became more. The first time he raped her, Sarah was twelve. A year later, he began selling her to his friends, and then to other men.

Once when Sarah had a bladder infection, she tried telling her mother what her uncle was doing, but her mother didn't believe her. She became angry that Sarah would say such incendiary things and accused Sarah of trying to ruin the good arrangement they had. Sarah's uncle was infuriated by the confession, and a few months later sold her to a pimp who moved her from Missouri to Florida — telling Sarah's mother she'd run off with an older guy who had a lot of money.

For the next ten years, Sarah was trapped in the commercial sex-trafficking industry with some time spent in jail and two years in prison. By the time, she reached her mid-twenties, she had a list of convictions, including numerous prostitution charges starting at age fifteen, as well as a felony for transporting minors across state lines for prostitution at the age of nineteen. Her pimp had put her behind the wheel to drive herself and the other young women to New Orleans to service the demand of men attending a Super Bowl game. He knew how to protect himself and received no jail time during her years with him.

Sarah was released from prison when she was twenty-one, and her pimp was waiting. By that time, Sarah viewed herself as a convicted prostitute. She had no other home to go to. A relative told her that her mom and uncle shared a house now. Sarah returned to her pimp. This time she began drinking heavily to stave off the pain and disgust over her life.

When Sarah found out she was pregnant, she was a twenty-four-year-old alcoholic and frequent drug user. She'd had two abortions before turning twenty. Sarah went to a clinic to get tested for HIV when she received the news that she was pregnant, and the nurse at the clinic seemed to care. She didn't treat Sarah like she was garbage. The older woman, Ruby, talked to her about prenatal care, taking vitamins with DHA for the baby's brain development, and about social services for pregnant women. Ruby didn't act as if Sarah deserved anything less than whatever helps were available. Ruby treated her like any pregnant woman who obviously needed guidance without judgment.

After Sarah left the clinic with a dozen fliers of information about programs and prenatal care in hand, Sarah couldn't stop thinking about the life inside her. In the bathroom, she leaned against the door and put her hand on her stomach wondering how big the baby had grown since the day before. If her pimp found out she was pregnant, she knew he'd force her to have another abortion. It happened often among the girls. The men didn't care to be careful.

Sarah knew this pregnancy was different. *She* was different because of it.

No matter how she felt about herself or how others saw her, Sarah had to get safely away from everything she knew … which was much easier said than done. Despite the darkness she lived in, this life was her home, and the other girls and her pimp were like an awful, dysfunctional, dangerous family. They were the only family she knew now.

Then she thought of that baby. Her baby.

The next morning, Sarah returned to the clinic and asked to talk to the nurse again. Ruby gave Sarah more specific help and the contact information for a friend who volunteered at a nonprofit organization that helped trafficking victims. Though she felt unsure and extremely afraid, the very idea of that baby growing inside her gave Sarah the strength to escape her pimp and get help.

In the months following, Sarah began counseling, started AA, and received prenatal care. She lived in a shelter until a bed opened at a house for survivors like her several states away. On the day she was given a sonogram, she cried — and sent the nurse, Ruby, a copy. When Millie was born, she told Ruby first and sent her pictures. They became friends on social media, and Sarah sent annual pictures to this woman, the one who told her later she prayed for

A SURVIVOR'S STORY

Sarah and her girls every day.

Soon Sarah had met someone who also attended AA —
someone she believed to be a great guy. But after dating for six
months, Sarah's new boyfriend, who told her he was divorced, broke
the news that he was going back to his wife. He was not interested
that the child she was now carrying in her womb was his.

While Sarah wanted to build a great life for her daughters,
doing so had proven difficult at every turn. She struggled to get a
job. She wanted to go back to school and earn her GED, maybe
even attend college ... but as a felon, she couldn't get financial aid.
Sarah's minimum-wage job wouldn't pay for school — she could
barely survive already. It had taken months of living in shelters and a
halfway house before Sarah found a one-bedroom place through the
nonprofit — otherwise, no one wanted to rent to her after asking
about criminal records and her credit score.

Sarah's involvement with the nonprofit led to her being
able to do trainings with law enforcement and local groups about sex
trafficking. At first, she was against the idea. She was a convict, after
all. But after some careful coaxing, Sarah attended the trainings and
did her part of the teaching. Once the first sessions were over, Sarah
realized how much she enjoyed it. She wondered how, if life had been
different, she might be teaching third grade right now.

One day at her job as hostess at a small family-owned
diner, Sarah shut down when the belligerent manager yelled at her
for something someone else forgot to do. She walked out of the
diner and lost her job. After that, Sarah struggled to find further
employment — also partially due to her past conviction and prison
time. Finally, the same nonprofit hired her part-time in the office,

and Sarah began to learn basic office skills to help her in the future.

Sarah's youngest daughter, Chloe, asked her weekly if she'd help in her classroom like the other moms. Sarah didn't know how to explain to her daughters that as a criminal and registered sex offender, she couldn't. Her past haunted (and still does) so many areas of her life.

Sarah also feels awkward in normal social situations. She knows she acts differently than the parents at her daughter's school. Sometimes she was plagued by uncertainty. She didn't want to be too loud or too quiet, too reactive or too passive. What if she did something socially abnormal that humiliated her daughters? Fear was a constant with her.

Just days before her birthday, Sarah heard about Vacatur laws that could clear her criminal record. She felt too afraid to hope it might be possible. If her past criminal records were vacated, doors would begin to open for her and her daughters, instead of the past constantly impairing her progress.

Now Sarah daydreams about all she could do if her criminal history was expunged. Mostly she imagines the look of surprise on Chloe's face when, coming in from recess at school, she sees her mommy finally helping in her class.

***

Sarah's story is a compilation of domestic minor sex trafficking victims who have been part of Shared Hope. Some have worked in our offices when they couldn't find another job. She represents so many women trying to create a good and safe life for herself and for her children. She wants to get over the pain and trauma of the past. She wants many things, and though right now most of her dreams are for her girls, lately the seeds of hope and dreams for herself have begun to grow.

Sarah's story signifies the importance of Vacatur laws.

18

CHANGING CULTURE, CHANGES LIVES

For good or ill, culture reflects the values held by a society. Sometimes there are big game-changers, but typically culture change happens slowly and incrementally, and often with much effort. When it comes to child sex trafficking in America, we recognized that many cultural corrections were needed to make an impact. Long-held beliefs, arcane procedures, and deficient laws all represented roadblocks to an accurate perception of the child sex trafficking victim. Changing the culture for survivors of this terrible crime would involve much effort, well beyond awareness — effort that would focus on making cultural corrections in three important areas:

- the language we use
- state laws to guide practices and perceptions
- and justice for victims

Changing Language

Language expresses and communicates culture. Even in different modes of language — such as texts, social media posts, and images that represent words or sayings — we are expressing culture. These words shape our perceptions and the way we view others around us. I realized that the words we used to discuss victims, justice, and the fight against trafficking had a huge impact on results and what's acceptable or not. The words we use to describe what is happening can either perpetuate apathy and prejudice or stir people to action.

Imagine this scenario: A *prostitute* gets a text from her pimp to meet on a side street for a blue SUV. She leans against a stone building in the middle of the night, shivering in a thin sweater. A vehicle pulls up under the streetlight at the end of the block, and she sees that it's the make and model that's been described in the text. The *prostitute* hops into the warm vehicle, but the driver insists on driving a few miles to a more secluded area before paying her for sex. She keeps her phone close and agrees to go. She'd rather take her chances with a stranger than go home without money. The SUV pulls away, and the *prostitute* is never seen again.

Now reread that same scenario and replace the word *prostitute* with the word *child*: A *child* gets a text from her pimp to meet on a side street for a blue SUV. She leans against a stone building in the middle of the night, shivering in a thin sweater. A vehicle pulls up under the streetlight at the end of the block, and she sees that it's the make and model that's been described in the text. The *child* hops into the warm vehicle, but the driver insists on driving a few miles to a more secluded area before paying her for sex. She keeps her phone close and agrees to go. She'd rather take her chances with a stranger than go home without money. The SUV pulls away, and the *child* is never seen again.

When you hear the word *prostitute*, what images come to mind?

Next, consider the image when you hear the words *child* or *domestic minor sex trafficking victim*.

Each word holds a meaning that, even in the same scenario, conjures up an entirely different picture. Words matter.

The power of words can build up and tear down. Our perception of the world is created through words. This topic of language has been foremost in how people can come to the aid of victims of child sex trafficking. We've worked hard to open eyes by calling out the need to change the words we use.

Imagine a police officer pulling up to a car parked in a desolate location. He sees two people inside it and investigates. He walks up to the car and finds them in the backseat — one is an older man, the other a young girl wearing makeup, and she's trying to cover herself up.

If a police officer sees the girl as a *child victim* in the backseat of that car, he will respond very differently than if he sees a *prostitute*. Once the word has changed, how will that *child* be treated? Not only does the police officer view the *child* or the

Is she a prostitute/whore/slut/working girl? Or a victim of child rape/kidnapping/assault?

If we start using accurate words to describe victims of domestic minor sex trafficking, would this change our culture? Our laws? The way we fight for justice?

prostitute very differently, so do prosecutors, judges, society, future employers, and, most importantly, that child herself.

I can't tell you the many hours I've discussed this topic with Ernie Allen, Drew Oosterbaan, Amy O'Neill Richard, Samantha Vardaman, Melissa Snow, and many others. We've talked about how people have justified children and minors being treated like prostitutes by saying things like:

> *She doesn't act like a child.*
> *She doesn't look like a child.*
> *She's not trying to get help.*
> *She acts guilty.*
> *She acts as if she wants to be there.*

Here's a fact: There is no such thing as "child prostitution."

We cannot connect those two words, "child" and "prostitute."

Many people are also unaware that a crime is committed when a person provides money or any other item of value in exchange for sexual interaction with a minor. That crime is sex trafficking.

From the Trafficking in Persons (TIP) office, "when a child (younger than 18 years of age) is recruited, enticed, harbored, transported, provided, obtained, patronized, solicited, or maintained to perform a commercial sex act, proving force, fraud, or coercion is not necessary for the offense to be characterized as human trafficking."

There are no exceptions to this rule — no cultural or socio-economic rationalizations alter the fact that children who are exploited for the sale of sex are trafficking victims. The use of children in the commercial sex trade is prohibited under U.S. law and by statute in most countries around the world.

CHANGING CULTURE, CHANGES LIVES

Prostitution should never be a word used to explain crimes against a child.

While words like *child prostitute* and *child prostitution* continue to be commonly used, the time for change has come.

People often ask what they can do to help in the battle against child sex trafficking. Changing how we talk about and refer to these kids will shape how they are viewed and how they are cared for. While it may seem minor, such a seemingly small change has wide-ranging impact — it's something all of us can do to create change and fight for some of the most vulnerable among us.

The Power of Accountability — Report Cards

We brainstormed with our fellow modern abolitionists on how to implement change at the local and state levels. With fifty states to tackle, we had to be strategic about how to encourage state and local governments to recognize the issue, create new procedures for helping child victims instead of arresting them as prostitutes, and pass laws that would prosecute buyers and traffickers.

Back on the day I met Samantha Vardaman and Drew Oosterbaan for coffee, an idea was born that would eventually become the Protected Innocence Challenge. I asked myself: *How best could we assess work, progress, performance, and conduct? Was there a way we did this in other areas of life?* And our conversation at Shared Hope centered around the question, "What would people understand?"

Eventually, we settled on an idea to create report cards for each state.

A report card made the most sense and would be understood widely. Even children understand report cards. The United States needed not just one report card, but one for every state. We decided the report card would grade the laws of each state on how well that state addressed child sex trafficking issues.

The grades were based on six key areas:

1. Criminalization of domestic minor sex trafficking victims — Were kids treated like criminals?

2. Criminal provisions assessing Demand — Were buyers of children being punished?

3. Criminal provisions for traffickers — Were traffickers of children being punished?

4. Criminal provisions for facilitators — Were facilitators of child sex trafficking being punished?

5. Protective provisions for child victims — Were the kids getting help?

6. Criminal justice tools for investigation and prosecution — Did a state have laws, procedures, and practices that were being used to put criminals away?

With their law degrees and expertise in child sex trafficking issues, Samantha Vardaman and Christine Raino, SHI's other invaluable attorney and senior director, created the framework for the Protected Innocence Challenge. Christine would go on to lead the annual reports. Director of Programs Melissa Snow would add her invaluable experience as well. To date, it is the only comprehensive study of U.S. state laws regarding child sex trafficking.

Since 2011, states have been graded every year on the way their laws are handling child sex trafficking within their borders. The report cards, issued by the Protected Innocence Challenge, are meant to provide a "challenge" for states to improve care of victims and justice against offenders, so recommendations for improvement are included. When we first issued the report cards, 26 states received a grade of F. As of 2016, there are no longer any states in the F category.

It has been an encouraging process to watch, but even more, it shows how the U.S. has not only been waking up to the issue of American kids being sold for sex, but the efforts to stop it have made significant headway as well.

The report cards are available annually on the Shared Hope website for anyone to see how their state is performing. It details where their home state is failing and where it's succeeding in the fight against child sex trafficking. Armed with this knowledge, citizens are able to educate themselves and join their voices with those of survivors who were previously hidden in the shadows.

Justice in Survivor Voices

As we've progressed in the fight against sex trafficking, survivors have been rising up to speak about their experiences — to be voices for those still enslaved. In the past, few survivors were given such opportunities. I see this as an amazing testimony of what restoration and justice provides these incredible individuals.

Shared Hope has provided networking, enrichment, and education opportunities for the survivor community for many years. Today survivors and survivor-informed organizations are taking a significant leading role in speaking publicly and training law enforcement, medical practitioners, hotel personnel, and others in the service industry. Many are influencing cultural change in the perception of a sex-trafficking victim through sharing their experiences via media.

In December 2015, President Obama made appointments of eleven members to be part of the U.S. Advisory Council on Human Trafficking.

This was a historic moment, as the members were comprised of survivors of human sex trafficking and labor trafficking. In this role, survivors have been able to advise and make recommendations to the President's Interagency Task Force (PITF) to monitor and combat trafficking in persons. Survivors have been allowed a voice and are placed in a position to offer significant input on federal anti-trafficking policies. As members, survivors actively:

- Provide advice and recommendations to the U.S. government, specifically the Senior Policy Operating Group (SPOG)[1] and the PITF, to strengthen federal policy and programming efforts that reflect best practices in the anti-trafficking field.
- Review federal U.S. government policy and programs intended to combat human trafficking, including programs relating to the provision of services for victims.
- Gather information from U.S. government agencies, states, and communities for the Advisory Council's annual report.
- Publish an annual report that contains the findings derived from the reviews conducted of federal government policy and programs.
- Serve as a point of contact for federal agencies reaching out to human-trafficking survivors for input on anti-trafficking programming and policies in the United States.
- Represent the diverse population of human-trafficking survivors across the United States.

During the President's Interagency Task Force meeting on January 5, 2016, the Advisory Council attended and participated in offering insights that cannot be understood by anyone except survivors.

Ms. Ima Matul Maisaroh spoke for the group by saying: "One key reason this Council is important is because it acknowledges the value that survivors add to any initiative on human trafficking. As a collective group of survivors, we have dedicated a huge part of ourselves to the anti-trafficking movement through our respective advocacy efforts. Together, we are changing perceptions, fighting for justice, and, ultimately, over the years, contributing to one shared goal — to end modern slavery everywhere it exists.

"We are a diverse group. Our individual experiences as survivors will add a richness of expertise to the Council, and we will act proudly as a united group of leaders who will speak up for what is needed to address the many issues that contribute to the long-standing existence of human trafficking in the United States and around the world."[2]

No one is more impacted by sex trafficking than the survivors. No one can speak about the issue or to other survivors better than they can. That survivors now have a voice at the federal level shows just how far we've come.

By changing our language, providing accountability to government on every level, and by giving survivors a voice at the highest level of our government, we are slowly but surely changing the culture of this nation for the better.

Now if we can just stop the demand.

[1] "U.S. Department of State. United States Advisory Council on Human Trafficking Annual Report 2016." https://www.state.gov/j/tip/263114.htm, October 18, 2016.

[2] "Trafficking in Persons Report 2016." Office to Monitor and Combat Trafficking in Persons. https://www.state.gov/j/tip/rls/tiprpt/2016/258689.htm.

19

ONLINE PREDATORS AND THE PORN CONNECTION

THE SHOCKING REALITY THAT THERE IS A MARKET FOR SEX WITH CHILDREN IS MADE ATROCIOUS BY THE INCREDIBLE VOLUME OF THIS DEMAND.

D emand.

When referring to demand in context of economics, it is defined as "the desire to purchase, coupled with the power to do so" and "the quantity of goods that buyers will take at a particular price."[1]

In domestic minor sex trafficking, demand means the desire to purchase American children for sex, coupled with the power to do so; and the quantity of American kids that buyers will take at a particular price.

The shocking reality that there is a market for sex with children is made atrocious by the incredible volume of this demand.

Despite our efforts, despite changes in laws and protocols,

despite awareness and services and restoration of survivors, the fact is Demand has increased.

As Chief at CEOS, Drew Oosterbaan and his team noticed a sudden rise in online images of children being sexually exploited. The forensic team had been working to rescue kids who were being victimized in pornographic pictures and videos for some time when Shared Hope began its research into DMST. They were training prosecutors on how to make cases and get convictions. They were getting things done. With this progress, it didn't make sense for the quick and incredible increase in Demand.

It didn't take long to figure out what was driving the Demand.

The Internet.

The connectivity of the World Wide Web created a new arena where crime and corruption flourished. Suddenly, it wasn't just pornography that was easily available to anyone with a computer and internet access; child pornography and finding out how to rent a child for sex became more accessible as well. We've talked about the porn connection and how it affects the brain and creates addiction that feeds into darker cravings. But there are also predators actively seeking you and your loved ones online, right now, every day.

The New Pimps

Online predators can stalk victims online and follow the tried-and-true methods of pimps who first become friends, then boyfriends, and eventually traffickers. They portray themselves as finding their soulmate online, and eventually, sometimes over the course of months to a year, they lure these girls and boys into commercial sex trafficking.

We are seeing more girls lured in by pimps posing as boyfriends via social media, dating sites, and other online means than through in-person meetings as was done in the past.

These kids are from every kind of family dynamic — yes, dysfunctional environments and lower-income bracket situations, but also from families who have actively protected their children.

Tactics for Future Demand

To keep industries profitable, new consumers must be created. In commercial sex trafficking, those consumers are future buyers of children for sex and for sexually exploited images. This is a money-making machine, and these businessmen/traffickers are cunning in their practices. They work hard to advertise and build on the demand today with an intention to create future consumers. They target your children. They target you.

Anyone who is on the Internet and accidentally happens upon an elicit image or chat offer has a high potential of being targeted. They send emails (often caught by spam folders, but not always) and social media messages as ways to connect with you, your spouse, your children, your parents, your friends.

Those ads at the bottom of news stories that catch your eye with a beautiful woman in a seductive pose … or that offer to show you something exciting, salacious, or gossipy … or an actual chat someone starts with you … or a communication meant to tempt you toward something just a little beyond what you'd normally do — these are intentional. This is marketing and advertising. Tactics like these are careful and progressive in luring people into the dark world of pornography, children in sexually exploited images (known as child porn), and eventually into purchasing sex with minors.

They are building Demand through you, and through your children. They are destroying minds, marriages, and families. People who started out like everyone else are lured in, become addicted, and some are now even going to prison. Lives are being destroyed for their profit.

What can we do to protect our kids?

What can we do against such a tide?

How can we protect our children?

How do we stop turning our little boys into men who buy sex in some form or another?

Parents are increasingly becoming more tech savvy, researching how to protect their children. By becoming active on social media and restricting apps that leave a child vulnerable to sexually explicit material, parents are taking control of what their little ones are exposed to and influenced by.

Other technology advances have created a market for apps that will help parents monitor their child's screen time. But parents must be ever vigilant.

The effects of sexually explicit material on a child's development are clear. Parents and other caring adults can protect our kids from porn. But what about all of the kids out there who don't have supervision?

We need schools, as well as outside groups and church organizations, to educate the kids. We tell the youngest of our children to not talk to strangers. We need a lot of discussion about the online strangers as well.

If we want to stop the demand for sex with children, we must keep doing more.

Tech Companies

Many organizations, including Shared Hope International, are urging tech giants like Facebook, Google, and YouTube to help in the fight against the commercial sexual exploitation of children. They have the power to do so! One example is found with UK tech companies that block pornographic material unless the patron wishes to receive it and intentionally "opts in." The practice, known as default filtering, is the direct opposite of the practice of U.S. tech companies that leave the porn floodgate wide open and push the responsibility of turning it off onto the user. Even without a change such as filtering, U.S. tech companies can make it easier to report and remove sexually explicit material, as well as providing the means to facilitate shutting down the intrusion on our personal devices.

Tech companies fear government control, and this is understandable. However, many of the laws meant to protect children against the dangers found online are also being translated by tech companies as a means of censorship and of the government trying to monitor the Internet — something they adamantly oppose.

There are also privacy issues to consider. What are the implications of monitoring what is posted, or law enforcement exploration of an individual's interactions on the Web? Yet in the midst of these considerations, one thing is clear: Children should not be for sale online, in any way. Stopping it, even in advance of resolving every privacy concern, should be the priority.

In the case of Backpage.com, the company claimed they weren't allowing children to be sold for sex through their website. Their "Adult" section was supposed to be for adults to interact with other adults in legal ways. They stated they were protecting against illegal and exploitative sexual abuses of children.

WHAT TECH COMPANIES CAN DO

- Enforce age verification — there are proven ways that age must be verified to enter sites that legally are for people over the age of 18.

- Instill warnings on searches and for illegal websites.

- Raise awareness — be part of helping people understand what is happening and how to stop it.

- Create parental guides for protecting kids online.

- Participate in new technologies that will help stop Demand, save children, and catch online predators.

- Install filters into search engines as is being done with Sky Network in Great Britain.

However, there was overwhelming evidence that Backpage.com was being used as a facilitator of online child sex trafficking — and was making an enormous profit as a result of these illegals ads, as well. Lawsuits were filed against the company by the parents of girls who were sold online through Backpage.com. Eventually, the site shut down its "Adult" section, but only after enormous legal and governmental pressure that included Senate hearings and arrest warrants.

This was a first victory, but progress is limited. The sale of kids for sex is big business.

Truths Most Want to Ignore

The exploitation of women and children is expressed both in the porn industry and in commercial sex trafficking.

Consumers of porn often believe, and want to believe, that "porn stars" are happy and enjoy the rich benefits of their work. The truth is, most adults in the porn industry live a dismal experience. The industry typically seeks young women in their late teens or early twenties. Few have a long career because they get "old." A high percentage have already been sexually abused and exploited. Many are or become drug addicts. Often these young women and young men have few options for financial survival or believe that they don't.

This is not what is touted by the media and by some of the stars themselves, though many later admit the dark truth of their experiences.

While "acting," these girls and boys, men and women, will experience sexual acts with strangers, often painful and degrading acts, and will usually catch a sexually transmitted disease.

These "stars" are not healthy and happy. They aren't independent people cherished by the porn industry. The business exploits the pain already found in their lives. Everyone is seeking love and acceptance, and for a time believe they may have found a sense of that by using their bodies in such a manner and without adverse effects. We all know this will not lead to joyful fulfillment.

When You View Porn — The Effects on Others

Viewing pornography may be a solo act; however, the production of the material and the social and relational consequences of the behavior extends far past the individual. Often children and adults endure brutal rape and abuse at the hands of pornographers and may require years of specialized therapy to heal from the intense trauma inflicted on them.

Trafficked women and children may face an increased risk of violence or degradation due to the normalization of deviant sex acts propagated through pornography.

If you view porn, you are creating Demand. You are responsible for the effects.

When You View Porn — The Effect on You

Pornography can skew your perception of healthy sexual behavior and boundaries. Real life sex becomes boring and does not satisfy as easily, often resulting in sexual dysfunction like erectile dysfunction in men or dissatisfying sex for both men and women. Porn can adversely impact your personal relationship with a spouse or significant other. It deteriorates your spiritual health as well.

If you are a man and your wife discovers a hidden porn habit, she can experience intense feelings of betrayal, loss of trust, a diminished sexual desire for you, and even crippling insecurities in herself.

When this occurs, a woman usually feels a sense of not being good enough for her husband. Some women may try to participate in porn to please a spouse, but it most often leads to further issues and the disintegration of marriage.

It's not only men who are addicted to pornography. Increasingly, women are viewing pornography online and experiencing personal consequences as well.

We Must Stop Demand!

We cannot give up on this fight to save minds, hearts, and

lives. The future of our children and our nation are at stake.

First, we must take personal responsibility. Do not view online porn or visit chatrooms or other online sites that advertise for these sites. If you have a habit or addiction, get help!

Next, some ways to stop demand are:

- Protect children from being lured into porn addiction
- Protect kids from being lured into becoming traffic victims
- Get tech companies to help
- Increase education and awareness for younger kids
- Support recovery programs that work for former buyers and for the victims
- Arrest and prosecute buyers
- Educate juries on the law
- Longer prison sentences for buyers
- Follow up on sex offender registration and monitoring
- Make buyers pay restitution to the victims

---

[1] Dictionary.com, https://www.dictionary.com/browse/demand.

20

The Forgotten Victims — Boys & Men

Judge Robert Lung

"... THERE IS A TERRIBLE LACK OF FOCUS ON MEN AND BOYS, WHICH TRANSLATES TO LACK OF SERVICES AND HELP."

JUDGE ROBERT LUNG

B oys are trafficked too.

This is easy to forget. In fact, it's easy to not consider it at all. When we think of trafficking victims, it's the girls and women who come to mind. Their images are what we normally see on online ads, on pamphlets handed out on the Vegas strip, or portrayed in news reports, movies, documentaries, and television shows.

We think of the men as the buyers, the pimps, or the traffickers. The victims are always female, the victimizers always male.

However, this is not true. Throughout the history of sex trafficking in the United States, boys and men have summarily been forgotten, ignored, or disregarded — even among the groups and departments trying to stop human trafficking.

As I've shared, I first became aware of commercial sex trafficking in an international setting. Later, after founding Shared Hope and digging into the research, my eyes were opened to what was happening on the streets of our own towns and cities in America. I was stunned by the scope and prevalence in our nation. At that time, I thought of it as a problem mainly for girls and women with a possibility of male victims as well, but that seemed the small minority. I wanted to focus on tackling the biggest problems to help the most people, which would eventually help everyone. It took additional time for us at Shared Hope to realize how big this issue is for boys too. Let me just say, it's enormous.

In 2014, I met Robert Lung. Officially, he's the Honorable Robert Lung, or Judge Lung. He has served on the bench for more than a decade and a half in the 18th Judicial District of Colorado. In 2016, he was appointed by the Colorado Supreme Court Chief

JUDGE ROBERT LUNG

In addition to presiding over a diversified docket in Colorado, Robert provides presentations nationally and internationally on issues such as human trafficking, childhood trauma, and resiliency. Judge Lung was recently appointed by the Colorado Supreme Court Chief Justice to serve as the Judicial Representative on the Colorado Human Trafficking Council. In 2016, he was selected to serve as a consultant to the Office for Victims of Crime (OVC) and as a consultant of the NHTTAC of the recently created Office of Tracking in Persons (OTIP) of the Federal DHHS. In 2017, Judge Lung was selected to

Justice to serve as the Judicial Representative on the Colorado Human Trafficking Council; he was selected in 2017 to serve on the National Advisory Committee on the Trafficking of Children and Youth in the United States; and in 2018, he was appointed to the U.S. Advisory Council on Human Trafficking. As a judge, Robert presides over a docket focused on kids experiencing trauma, neglect, abuse, and family issues.

Robert and I were attending an event for sex-trafficking survivors when we first met. Robert was another speaker, and we were staying at the same hotel when we recognized each other at the hotel restaurant. As we struck up a conversation, Robert immediately made an impact on me as he shared how boys and men were terribly underserved and under-represented in the movement. He was trying to change that.

When you meet Robert, you are immediately impressed by him. He's engaging, charismatic, and caring, and his career

serve as a member of the National Advisory Committee on the Sex Trafficking of Children and Youth in the United States, which will advise the U.S. Attorney General and the Secretary of the U.S. Department of Health and Human Services on trafficking. Most recently, in 2018, Judge Lung was appointed by the President to the nine-member U.S. Advisory Council on Human Trafficking tasked to advise the President's Interagency Task Force to Monitor and Combat Trafficking in Persons (PITF). Judge Lung received a triple-major B.A. from Regis University and his J.D. from the University of Dayton. He is also currently working on his first book, a biography of trafficking, trauma, resiliency, faith, and, above all else, hope.

is impressive. You would never expect that Robert is also a sex-trafficking survivor.

In 2013, Robert began to talk publicly about childhood trauma, including his own. As a child, Robert was trafficked by his father. His own history paired with a career seeing the egregious lack of services for boys has propelled Robert to speak for those who can't speak themselves.

I'll never forget when Robert was one of our speakers at a JuST (Juvenile Sex Trafficking) Conference. In one segment, a group of trafficking survivors were on stage and photographs were displayed on the screen showing two photos of each person. One photograph showed each survivor today, and one was a childhood photograph of the age when they were trafficked.

It was heartbreaking to see the photographs of those innocent children knowing the horrific abuse that had happened to them. Ten of the survivors were women, and two were men. Robert was one of them.

When the photo came to the first male survivor and shifted to the image of a little boy sitting in a chair, I heard a gasp through the whole room even though the audience had already been viewing and moved by the female survivors' photos. Then Robert's photograph was shown and then shifted to him as a boy around grade school. The gasp in the room turned to a moan. As heartbreaking as all of the photos were, the images of little boys being trafficked had a much stronger gut reaction in the audience. Some people couldn't even look. I saw them turn away.

I felt this experience represented our society in many ways. We have such a hard time looking at the boys as victims. It's more shocking. It's also part of the reason why there are so few men who will step up and speak about their abuse. They don't want to be seen as weak or bad or victims, or to have people look away. That reaction represented to me what America feels toward the male survivors. Shocked or unable to see them.

It's rare to find a man like Robert with the courage to bring out his childhood trauma and also to speak up for other victims everywhere. I'll let Robert tell you more of his story ...

***

I hadn't planned to become a speaker and advocate for boys and men. In fact, I had no plans of ever publicly revealing what had happened to me as a child. My interest was in the law.

I first became fascinated by the law during high school when I had this great teacher who taught constitutional law. He made the law interesting, relevant, and compelling — he challenged us to understand it and then debate it amongst ourselves in every class. The more I learned, the more I loved it — from the development of law itself and how it's refined year after year by the courts and the process of laws to how everything is controlled or modified by law. There isn't anything in the world that isn't touched by it. Our food, our beds, our homes, where we live, and how we own property, the air we breathe, even our religions and how we practice our faiths are protected or modified by the law. Everything is influenced by the law.

Later, I discovered more about the courts and the process of litigation. I like to explain litigation like this: two sides (opposing parties) are trying to piece together a jigsaw puzzle for the court. Neither side has all the pieces — if they did, the other side would concede and they'd settle out of court. Instead, both sides are trying to piece the puzzle together the best they can. Whether it's by a jury or a judge, the decision to be made is whose puzzle fits together best. All of it is this amazing, magical, and yet logical, methodical process.

As I went into law, it led me into cases that I wanted to do something about. Child trauma cases were something I understood. Hardly anyone knew this at the time, but I had my own childhood trauma that I'd kept hidden for years.

When people look at my life or career from the outside, no one would imagine the trauma I experienced from the time I was very young until my mid-teens. I seem to have it all together. I've been on an upward trajectory in my career. I do not look or act like what people imagine of a trafficking survivor — especially a *male* trafficking survivor.

My father was a very intelligent and successful doctor, an oral surgeon to be exact, who owned several offices around the Midwest city where I grew up. We were an upper-class family and looked really good on the outside. My father was a master at covering up his deeds when he wanted to; my mother never knew, and he threatened my life to keep me silent. Since he was a doctor, I believed my father when he said he could kill me and no one would ever know he'd done it. He sometimes demonstrated exactly how, and he terrified me. It was more proof than I needed to keep quiet and bury the trauma deep inside.

I can't say that nobody knew about the dark side of my father, because quite a few people certainly did. The other people who knew were men — pedophiles who traded young boys between each other, stealing their innocence and destroying their childhoods for their own despicable and twisted pleasure.

Eventually, I entered high school and became an age no longer desirable for men like my father. Looking back, I realize the fact that I survived is remarkable, if not miraculous.

For many years, there was no room for the horrors of childhood as I went off to college, dove into my studies and the law, and even after my father died unexpectedly of a heart attack. Still it was buried deep.

Eventually it caught up, and there have been points over the years that it's been the kind of thing that takes you out at your knees. Even when I've thought I was past it, the memories would still flood back … like when my own sons became the same age I had been when the abuse began. I realized how innocent and young I really was, and what a monstrous thing my father had done to me. When my youngest son was being treated for leukemia, I had to help hold him down while he was screaming during a medical procedure. Flashbacks barreled over me as I remembered being held down and screaming in pain. I knew in my mind that it wasn't anything like what I'd experienced — that we were trying to save my son's life, and he needed shots and IVs to do that. Still, my heart and soul felt crushed by those awful moments. These were some of my hardest moments.

When I went into law and my career really started, I worked for the District Attorney's Office, in the Child Support Enforcement Division. The last thing I wanted anyone to know was that I had childhood trauma of my own. I was fearful that they would question my authenticity or motivation, that I might be considered biased and discounted because of it.

I went years without talking to anyone about it. It wasn't something I wanted to tell anyone, especially when I became a judicial officer. People might question if I could be fair and impartial, that I might be biased against defendants.

Then in 2013, I started speaking about childhood trauma. I wasn't a judge yet, I was a District Court Magistrate — a big difference. I went to a colleague and asked, "If I go here, if I give these presentations and come out as a survivor, do you think it's going to cost me my chance at becoming a judge?"

My colleague Judge Larry Bowling answered, "There certainly is that risk. It's a matter of what's more important to you."

I was like, "Thanks, Larry ... thanks for the non-answer." But really, he was right. I had to decide what was most important to me: my career or making a difference.

Or was it possible to pursue both goals?

As I thought it over, I considered the absence of any positive information — anything about recovery, resiliency, and overcoming trauma. When you attend these conferences about child trauma or sex trafficking, the stories are heartbreaking — they're horrific. However, I had a story of hope. I wanted to bring that hope to the movement. I also felt that if God gave me the ability to live through my childhood, it had to be for more than just living through it. I'd survived in spite of life. Now I get to live for something else.

I had also discovered the terrible under-representation of male sex-trafficking victims and survivors. Nobody knew about us. That had to change.

It was during law school when I was forced to deal with my childhood abuse. My father was already dead, and I couldn't run from it any longer. While therapy was and still is an invaluable help, I also sought other resources. But there weren't any for men.

I remember going to a bookstore searching for something on the subject of boys being trafficked. There was very little available on the subject of trafficking in the first place at the time — only one book at the bookstore, and it was focused solely on girls and women. I tried reading through the book by changing the reference from female to male since there was nothing for boys and men, but it was very clearly directed toward women. This is a recurring theme I still see today. There's so very little for boys and men.

At that time, I believed there was no one else out there with a story like mine. Yet while my childhood has a lot of unique elements, such as incest and torture, the number of boys in sexual abuse and trafficking situations is a staggering amount. It's not a rare occurrence. There are *many* boys and men who've experienced abuse similar to what I did. People just don't think of boys and men as sex-trafficking victims or survivors. People don't *want* to think of it. Yet it's undeniable that boys and men are severely underserved and rarely recognized.

That's when I decided to step forward and tell people what happened to me.

My first presentation in 2013 was only about childhood trauma. It took me time to begin adding, more specifically, my own personal trafficking trauma history in my presentations, but still I didn't emphasize how underserved and unrecognized boys and men are in trafficking. Then, I decided to include an "anonymous" case study in my talk about a boy experiencing trafficking and childhood trauma. I wanted a case study to help those in the audience understand and feel what a child experienced. At the end of my presentation, I revealed that I was the subject of the case study.

Finally, I was telling my story, and it began in earnest at a Juvenile Sex Trafficking (JuST) Conference in Washington, D.C., hosted by Shared Hope International.

I specifically started talking about trafficking of boys and men in 2017, often at the request of the host at whose venue I was speaking. This was no easy task at first — it felt like being exposed in a way. But it also became liberating for me. During these talks, I also began to include the vast sexual discrimination that I've discovered toward men on this issue.

Now I don't want to come across as being against helping girls and women; not at all. My messages are about hope, prospects, and something positive. I don't want to take anything away from girls and women. In fact, I point out during my presentations that the progress and significant advantages for girls and women serve as the horizon that men and boys can point to — not *instead* of the girls, but *with* them. I want everyone to get the help they need. I simply seek equal assistance.

But the fact is, there is a terrible lack of focus on men and boys, which translates to lack of services and help.

The numbers vary on just how many minor trafficking victims are male. A study in New York found that 44.5 percent of trafficked youth were boys. Other studies have reported similar numbers. There are some studies that greatly contradict these, and people sometimes criticize these numbers.

I question why they want to criticize it. I'm curious about

the motivations of organizations that criticize and try to make it seem like it's a small number of boys. Why minimize the number of boys and men who need services as a result of their trafficking victimization experiences? Far more importantly, we need to understand the message such a stance sends to traffickers. If the message to traffickers is that we, as a society, are going to ignore or minimize boys and men, the traffickers will victimize more boys and men — the invisible, ignored, and abandoned victims of society.

The statistics I received out of Colorado in 2017 from the FBI's Rocky Mountain Safe Streets Innocence Lost Task Force were that 18.5 percent of rescued youth were boys. The bottom line in all of these numbers is this: We still have a huge percentage of the victim population not being recognized or rescued.

If you search for "youth trafficking" online, you'll find that 99 percent of the images are female. A law professor, Samuel Vincent Jones, wrote a piece called *The Invisible Man: The Conscious Neglect of Men and Boys in the War on Human Trafficking*. He wrote how in 2009 the Department of Justice and the U.S. Agency for International Development provided federal funding to 222 domestic and international institutions and programs to combat trafficking. Of those 222 groups, only two were male-orientated. That's less than 1 percent of help going toward boys and men when they represent at least 18 percent and up to 44.5 percent of the victims. How can this be justified or defended? If the "shoe were on the other foot," would women be okay if they received less than 1 percent of the federal funding to combat their victimization while they comprised 20 to 40 percent of the victim population? It's not right and it must change.

Why don't we know about the boys?

For one, the stories sit with people differently. It seems easier for society to imagine girls and women as victims of sexual violence than boys and men.

Men are less likely to talk about their childhood trauma, and particularly about sexual abuse and trafficking. Men are often more shamed over what they've experienced than women because our culture has such a hard time imagining males as victims. That's not how our culture perceives or wants to perceive men, and so the culture doesn't welcome this. We were all raised in a John Wayne culture — our image of men depicts riding horses, shooting guns, and not being victims of anything. But the fact is, boys and men need help too.

I often hear the same reasons over and over again for why boys are not being helped. "Oh, yeah, we should do something about boys, but we don't even know where to start or what to do."

I have a simple answer: Do the exact same thing you're doing for the girls. Everything being done for girls can be done for boys. There isn't a special service or treatment. Cognitive behavioral therapy works for girls, and guess what? It works for boys as well. Every treatment a girl can receive a boy can receive. You aren't treating their gender; you are treating their victimization.

Not knowing what to do is an excuse that just doesn't fly.

After getting past the surprise, "Oh, boys are trafficked too?" the next step should be, "Let's provide the exact same services currently existing for girls and make a significant difference."

What we need to remember is that there is hope. I always want to return to that message. We can make changes. We can reshape this conversation and educate people on what is really happening. We can use therapies and services that take traumatized people — both male and female — and give them the tools to build new lives. There is a great need for services for boys, and I am hopeful there are nonprofits out there courageous enough to fill the gap and answer the pleading, and yet unanswered call, of trafficked boys. I am aware of three organizations providing direct services or housing for boys: Courtney's House in Washington, D.C., United States Institute Against Human Trafficking in Florida, and the Ark of Freedom Alliance in Florida. I am aware of two organizations providing or preparing to provide services to boys: Restore One in North Carolina and The B.U.D.D.Y. House, Inc. in Georgia. These great nonprofit organizations are courageously addressing services to trafficked boys and men. However, with only five nonprofits in the whole country, is that the best we can do? My hope is the horizon set by the services available for girls and women may one day be achieved for trafficked boys and men, and that a list will come into existence that reflects service providers in every state in the country.

When I was interviewed by the Colorado Governor's office to become a judge, they asked whether I thought my experiences as a child could impair my ability to be fair and impartial. I quoted famous American jurist Oliver Wendell Holmes, Jr.: "The life of the law has not been logic; it has been experience … it cannot be dealt with as if it contained only the axioms and corollaries of a book of mathematics" (*The Common Law*, 1881, pg.1). I explained that I believed it improved my ability to be fair and impartial because I had a deeper insight into the lives of trauma-impacted people and a more diverse experience of life than most.

I'd thought a lot about this, and I knew that instead of being biased, I was actually better equipped to be in the roles in which I was serving. It's what I consider a different depth of understanding. And the fact of the matter is, all of my perpetrators have passed away. I'm not presiding over my childhood experiences. The resolution of the cases that I deal with aren't going to change the past. But I believe my life experiences foster a keener insight and enhance my ability to perceive the nuances in the particular cases before me.

What I don't leave behind while on the bench is compassion and hope. In cases involving the local Department of Human Services in which child abuse or neglect is alleged, I truly feel compassion and hope for everyone in the case, including the accused. The purpose of the case is to improve the lives of children with a strong deference to reunification and strengthening of the family unit, however unique the concept of 'family' might be in some cases. If the case is successful, those accused parents may become the best parents ever. If the parents prove incapable or unwilling to change their neglectful or abusive behaviors, we will still improve the lives of the children by finding them a safe and nurturing home, preferably with protective and loving relatives. I have

WHAT CAN HELP?

By Judge Lung

Childhood trauma is repairable. Science shows that every part of us is repairable, especially the brain. There is hope for both male and female survivors. It's not an easy road, but I'm proof that it's possible. This certainly depends on severity of trauma, but here are some basics that helped me:

- **Peers, family, and good relationships**

- **Basic talk therapy (telling your story) is important**

also presided over cases involving trafficked youth struggling with their own cases, and while I don't disclose about my personal experiences, I am able to reach the youth and communicate to them in a manner that, I believe, let's them know I hear, I understand, and I care. And whether it is the accused parent, the abused child, or the trauma-impacted trafficked youth, I believe when they experience hope and receive compassion in the courtroom their prospect for meaningful change increases dramatically.

- **Group Therapy — learning you are not alone**
- **Cognitive Behavioral Therapy and Dialectical Behavioral Therapy**
- **Eye-Movement Desensitization Reprocessing (EMDR)**
- **Interpersonal therapy combined with medication (time-limited, not dependent)**
- **Non-traditional, supplemental methods: yoga and massage therapy (though both can be triggering), acupuncture, energy work such as Reike, aromatherapy to assist in grounding during a triggering event, and exercise.**

Since connecting with Shared Hope International and other organizations, I see how important it is for each of us to serve our paths well. Linda and I have different origin paths. She sees big picture and is part of changing laws and policies, among all of Shared Hope's other work. As a judge, I appreciate that, because when I'm on the bench, I can only help kids to the extent that the law allows me in each particular case. I must follow the law, so we need the law to offer the best avenues for children.

And because of my origin, my path is two-fold: First, engage the state and federal government along with nonprofit organizations to combat human trafficking, and second, engage the parties in my cases to foster meaningful change and improve the lives of children. Along the way, I have accepted the burden of carrying a banner on behalf of boys and men — they need and deserve the same resources as girls and women in their journeys to recovery. It took some time to be ready to speak about it and hold up this banner, but now it's what I'm meant to do.

THE FORGOTTEN VICTIMS — BOYS & MEN

21

THE SEX TRAFFICKING MOVEMENT FROM A SURVIVOR'S PERSPECTIVE

Kristy Childs

"THE REAL EXPERTS ABOUT SEX TRAFFICKING AND COMMERCIAL SEX EXPLOITATION ARE THE SURVIVORS."

KRISTY CHILDS

I first met Kristy Childs back in the early 2000s. Our staff at Shared Hope was making an inventory of other individuals and organizations who were working to combat sex trafficking around the country. There weren't all that many at that time, and there certainly wasn't someone like Kristy.

When we heard about the work she was doing, and also that she was a survivor, we were completely floored and impressed. Most women never escaped "the life," as Kristy called it, and even fewer were able to successfully rebuild their lives if they did. Kristy not only had done both of those, she'd also dedicated herself to the work of helping other women and children still out on the streets.

I flew to Kansas City, Missouri, to meet this woman who was working out of a basement helping people who had been or were in prostituted situations. I didn't really understand all that she was doing until I walked down into that basement.

At that time, Kristy had already started Veronica's Voice, a nonprofit offering help to girls and women on the street. We met at the old church that was giving her space to work. I remember descending into that leaking basement — some workers were trying to fix it.

Kristy is smart and articulate. She's a no-nonsense, get-things-done type of person. It was immediately clear to me that she had something great to offer the world. Talking to her, hearing her express what women and children on the streets needed, greatly affected me. I saw there were things Shared Hope couldn't do, and shouldn't do. However, with Kristy being a survivor and truly understanding, she could directly influence women in ways no one else could.

The mission of Veronica's Voice is poignant because Kristy knows the horrors of being trafficked as a child and continuing in the commercial sex industry into adulthood because hope and help appeared unavailable and out-of-reach. Kristy understands because she's been there. The mission of Veronica's Voice is to empower women to exit from, to prevent entry into, and to end all demand for prostitution/sex trafficking in the United States through survivor leadership.

Kristy became one of the first survivors to be a voice and example in the world, helping other victims who remain in the life and assisting those who want to escape and rebuild their lives.

It hasn't been an easy road as Kristy will share. But it's an admirable one. Nearly twenty years later, she's still making an impact in the world.

***

As a sex industry survivor, I have always been "on the front lines" of the movement to educate people about commercial sex exploitation (CSE). Furthermore, Veronica's Voice (VV), the organization I founded to help women and girls who want to exit CSE, is now eighteen years old. As a result, I have participated in and observed many developments in the sex-trafficking (ST) movement. Fortunately, I had invaluable help along the way, especially from the Sisters of Charity of Leavenworth, Shared Hope International, and countless individuals.

Although groups like VV have come a long way, we still have a great distance to go. It's critical that survivors are heard in this movement, not just for our stories and insights or as "token" survivors. We must also be heard to inform individuals and organizations about issues that still need to be addressed, but I'll get to all of that soon.

My Personal Story

I was trapped in CSE for twenty-four years, starting when I

ran away from home at twelve and ending at the age of thirty-six —
when I turned my last and final trick.

I couldn't find a way out.

At the point when suicide was my only option to get out, I
received a miracle and was given the ability to see the steps to exit
from "the life." That miracle happened when I was almost thirty, and
it took me six years to completely exit. Yes, I had to prostitute myself
out of prostitution, like many of us have and many still must. You
see, in 1992, there was no place for someone with my history to get
assistance. I also had no trust in any of the governmental or nonprofit
systems that had already failed me and criminalized me. Far too many
times, individuals within those systems also sexually exploited me.

Once I was out and had the skills to obtain a job in which I
made a living wage, my mind wouldn't let go of the ones left behind.
I knew I needed to create a safe place for them. My vision: long-term
housing where survivors could get the trauma therapy needed, obtain
marketable skills, and find jobs with living wages. Also, I recognized
there was (and still is, in many places) a great deal of public ignorance
about prostitution; I wanted people to understand what prostitution
really is, as well as the conditions that lead girls and women (mostly)
into this violent, almost inescapable subculture.

Up to this point in my life, I had not been open about my
history. Most survivors knew better than to let others know our
past. Our time hadn't come yet. In fact, it remains unclear whether
or not our time has come now. Survivors are still often exploited by
people wanting to make a name for themselves in the movement.
This issue — academics, researchers, and other professionals
exploiting survivors while simultaneously claiming they work with

us — has become a topic in literature about ethics when dealing with vulnerable populations (which by definition includes prostitution survivors).

After working several years at the Kansas City Area Chamber of Commerce, I went to Sister Linda Roth who had developed a program, Keyboards to Success — a computer and job readiness course at the nonprofit El Centro. This is where I received training that catapulted me into the mainstream workforce.

I later shared with Sister Linda that I wanted to update my resume and look for another job. She asked, "Would you be interested in working for me as a case manager?"

"Of course," I said. Then one day while having lunch together, I began to share my story with Sister Linda — my life in prostitution for twenty-four years, what her program had done for me, and my vision of a different world for women and girls in the life. That conversation was the beginning of a new life for me.

Veronica's Voice

Several weeks later, Sister Linda walked by my desk and said, "You're going to get a call about a job that has your name written all over it." The call came a few days later — the Sisters of Charity of Leavenworth (in Kansas) were giving $25,000 in seed funding to start a program for prostituted women. I couldn't believe it! I thought it was going to be something for troubled kids. *No one was doing anything for adult women experiencing prostitution!*

I began speaking at several area churches, asking for toiletries and other personal care items, and making outreach bags in my dining room. Then I hit the streets. I had originally called

the organization "Veronica's Ministry," named after my friend
from the streets whom I met when she was only fourteen. Veronica
Neverdusky was brutally murdered at the age of twenty-one. To this
day, I believe Veronica's spirit is one of the forces guiding me.

I learned through doing outreach as "Veronica's Ministry"
that the name wasn't quite right yet. The prostituted women I came
in contact with assumed I represented a religious organization. They
put on a mask for me, like saying "Oh, thank you. God bless you."
Their responses were not authentic. I knew these women were already
wearing masks for others and wanted them to have a safe place to be
real. I quickly changed the name to "Veronica's Voice." I also secured
various locations to offer support groups.

Eventually, in my search for spiritual and emotional support,
I ran across survivor Norma Hotaling, in San Francisco, who had
founded an organization called SAGE (Standing Against Global
Exploitation). My excitement about meeting her and others like me
was almost uncontainable. Again, I had never met anyone who had
escaped the life alive.

Norma was a great resource to me. She was the leading
survivor voice in the emerging "Human Trafficking" or "Sex
Trafficking" movement. It was through Norma that I met other
survivors who worked for her and still more who were activists here
in America: Vednita Carter, founder of Breaking Free in Minnesota;
Kathleen Mitchell, founder of Dignity House, a program of the
Catholic Charity Services in Arizona; and Dr. B. Julie Johnson in
Illinois. We survivors knew our purpose: we had to be the ones to
educate mainstream society since we were the only ones who could
truly understand CSE. Several years later, I was introduced to Rachel

Lloyd, founder of GEMS in New York, and Tina Frundt, who eventually founded Courtney's House in Washington, D.C.

A View of the Movement

What I say here is my personal perspective as a survivor, advocate, and service provider.

While survivors have mostly welcomed the federal Trafficking Victims Protection Act (TVPA, 2000, and its subsequent reauthorizations), some of us in the grassroots movement have become acutely aware of what's effective and what's not. There are several issues that need to be addressed; due to time and space constraints, I will only name the most important.

There are huge problems due to the following converging factors: TVPA is federal law, but the states enforce it according to their own rules. There is still widespread public ignorance about commercial sexual exploitation and much debate around it; various "leaders" in the movement have exploited (stolen) survivors' work and voices — even those in positions to become leaders themselves — and some have actively tried to silence those whose ideas about CSE differ in any way from their own.

Overall, ideological extremism fosters greater misunderstanding about the issues and hurts survivors, including those still in CSE. For example, when people refer to all prostitution as "slavery" (even though some of it is), or when their opponents say those who don't view prostitution as "empowering" are moralistic and not "sex positive," this 1) ostracizes and polarizes women still in the industry, and 2) causes important actors in the movement (like government officials) to be misguided. Consequently, there are great variations in the way (or even whether) states distinguish between child and adult CSE.

And of course, we have well-known organizations like Amnesty International and the United Nations officially recommending that CSE should be decriminalized across the board.[1] Amidst all the lingering ignorance about CSE — and those capitalizing on such ignorance to make careers for themselves — is it any wonder?

Impact of TVPA and State Law

TVPA — written by non-survivors — ushered in language changing "commercial sexual exploitation" to "sex trafficking." First, this ostracized the very women I was seeking to help. They didn't identify with the term "sex trafficking" (and many still don't).

Second, the federal law requires *proof* of force, fraud, or coercion to meet the definition of "sex trafficking." Unfortunately, most women in CSE are so accustomed to abuse and exploitation, they, for the sake of survival, have normalized it in their minds. Hence, they often don't recognize it.

Example: When an exited friend of mine went to talk with two attorneys about sex exploitation by a professional, she was confused — after answering their questions for nearly four hours — when one said, "It's very clear from the way you talk that you have experienced a lot of sexual abuse." She wondered, *Gee, what did I say that led him to say that?* Even after being out of the industry for eight years, this woman didn't recognize that her commercial sexual exploitation was sexual abuse! Adding to this kind of confusion, prostituted women have been, and still are, treated as "criminals."

And lastly, on top of all this, our society glamorizes and/ or normalizes their abuse while simultaneously scorning them as citizens.

I also began to notice serious problems in enforcement of TVPA that actually re-victimize victims. In some states, for example, charges of prostitution are expunged if the person can prove she or he was a trafficking victim; in other states, juveniles beaten and heinously abused by pimps (traffickers) are arrested as co-conspirators as soon as they turn eighteen. Furthermore, in some states, authorities enforce TVPA by charging victims as conspirators with their perpetrators, even when these cases involve girls who were underage when their pimps found them and began to brainwash them. The kids learn if they don't "obey" they will be beaten, humiliated, or killed. Later, as adults, rather than "disobeying" after reaching age eighteen, they pay the price of spending years or even decades in prison.

Additionally, in many cases under the eyes of the law you are a "worthy victim" if you provide a case for the government; that is, if the government "certifies" you as a trafficking victim and, perhaps more importantly, if you will provide testimony against your abuser/ trafficker. In the world I came from, these perpetrators are pimps, and you don't want to go against them, because that's when the situation gets very dangerous. It's similar to battered women trying to leave their abusers.

This, by the way, is only one of the problems of 1) using age as an artificial distinction between "worthy victims" and "criminals;" 2) having unresolved conflicts between federal law and state law; and 3) reinforcing the notion that "choice" — in the traditional, rational sense of the word — is consistently found among people over eighteen in the sex trade.

Prostitution, commercial sex exploitation, sex work — whatever you want to call it — is only a *choice among very limited choices*.[2] Think about people in a rapidly burning high rise apartment. If they "choose" to jump to their deaths instead of returning inside to die by fire, is that a real "choice"?

However, we are currently witnessing the spread of the de-contextualized use of "force" vs. "choice," not only in government but also in NGOs and the general public. Even some NGO service providers are now eliminating services to women in prostitution who don't self-identify as trafficking victims.[3]

The philosophy at Veronica's Voice is that we believe anyone involved in CSE for any reason who wants out — regardless of how they identify, including as "sex workers" — deserves and should receive services to assist them in exiting. We do not view prostitution as a job, but we respect and honor victims'/survivors' choices about language. Anyone who comprehends anything about sex trauma knows it is of paramount importance to give power back, *not take it away*.

A related problem is pressuring victims and even threatening to charge them with trafficking (yes, this happens) if they don't assist prosecutors by testifying against their perpetrators. It's flat out wrong. It is re-victimizing. Many are simply not ready to face such a challenge; some have even been killed or otherwise endangered because somewhere between actions taken by the feds and the states, no one protected them.[4]

Reporter Jonathan Shorman writes, "Dozens of possible child trafficking victims have been jailed in Kansas."[5] Based on

Kansas Department for Children and Families data, *The Wichita Eagle* reported, "One in five possible child victims assessed by rapid response teams from 2014 to 2018 were in juvenile detention. In eastern Kansas, juvenile detention was the most frequent housing option for possible trafficking victims." This continues to occur despite universal acknowledgement that such detention is detrimental.

A case in point is that of Hope Joy Mae Zeferjohn, whose situation Elizabeth Nolan Brown described objectively: "A teenage runaway being threatened by a violent older pimp, Hope Zeferjohn should have been saved when Topeka police arrested the man for human trafficking. Instead, she was cast as a conspirator in his schemes and now faces more than a decade in prison."[6]

It didn't matter that at the time her violent pimp found her (she had left him, had given birth, and was doing well with her educational goals), police had issued an order of protection against him. Only by violating that did he get to her. Reportedly he did more than sweet talk to get her back; he beat her. And it didn't matter that Hope was technically a child, underage, when he cajoled her into his service. No — none of that mattered. As soon as the girl turned eighteen, the court designated her as the pimp's accomplice.

Try to imagine experiencing repeated rapes and beatings, often unpredictably. Now close your eyes and imagine you're behind bars, for a long time — and because of officials' confusion and public ignorance, you yourself are labeled as a conspirator with your rapist. I view this as state sponsored violence against already traumatized victims, and all states need to fix this *now*. But also, TVPA must become more specific in its directions to arresting officers and state court authorities.

Another problem we face: legitimizing commercial sex businesses by allowing them to form nonprofits, who then position themselves — through the Department of Homeland Security (DHS) — as partners against trafficking.[7] This totally separates CSE from Trafficking. Consider COAST (Club Operators Against Sex Trafficking). COAST is made up of multiple "gentlemen's clubs" — and is now directly aligned with DHS.

Furthermore, ex-strippers who identify as survivors because of the commercial sexual exploitation they experienced are not "trafficked" according to the legal definition in TVPA. Yet most strippers note that stripping is extremely exploitive, and a favored method of many pimps to coerce entry into prostitution.

When DHS partners with COAST, it honestly reminds me of George Orwell's book *1984*, or Margaret Atwood's *The Handmaid's Tale*: in both, language has become meaningless because of the elite's backlash against vulnerable people trying to fight for their rights. For example, in Orwell, you'll find statements like "Freedom is Slavery." In Atwood's book, the elite males are superficially devoted to their wives and against infidelity but then visit establishments where they interact with poor women who function as "entertainers." Our language: "Gentlemen's Clubs."

What COAST and DHS are doing severely damages the fight against commercial sexual exploitation. It is a very sly and cunning move on the part of the legal pimps — profiteers of the flesh trade, if you will.

Why can't we pass laws in which all sexually oriented businesses must have culturally sensitive posters in the dressing rooms as well as throughout the establishment about sex trafficking? The law could also require training that all employees, including the owner, would have to take on a yearly basis, that clearly describes various elements of coercion. Now, though, it's almost as if our government is teaching "how to profit most and look good while marketing in women's bodies."

Importance of the Survivor Voice

While some organizations have been instrumental in furthering the anti-trafficking movement and helping victims — Shared Hope being one of them — other individuals and organizations, including sometimes our own government, have left damage behind them. The real experts about sex trafficking and commercial sex exploitation are the survivors; our voices have been largely left out and/or manipulated in others' interest.

We are the ones who have a real choice: we can turn all this around or we can witness our groundbreaking efforts fizzle out and leave no lasting changes. The direction we need to be taking is adopting the Nordic Model, but with *primary emphasis on helping those who want out and creating alternatives for them*. It's one thing to pass laws addressing mass sexual exploitation (yes,

The Nordic Model is an approach to prostitution that decriminalizes those who have been prostituted. It provides support services to help them leave prostitution and criminalizes buying people for sex in order to reduce the demand that drives sex trafficking. This approach has now been adopted in Sweden, Norway, Iceland, Northern Ireland, Canada, France, and Ireland.

that's what it is at this point in history). The real challenge lies in creating economic and social environments in which underprivileged and marginalized individuals will not be forced by circumstance to "choose," if you will, commercial sex. We cannot end child trafficking while normalizing the industry for others to be consumed who happen to be over eighteen.

The U.S. has set a standard for the world with TVPA, and yet we are still arresting and criminalizing survivors. Why?

I thank Shared Hope for the opportunity to present this chapter, and my survivor colleague, Julie Johnson, Ph.D, for her editorial assistance.

***

As a survivor, Kristy Childs knows how to fight and overcome. She's had to use those skills to make Veronica's Voice successful against the many challenges she's faced and to be effective in reaching other people still trying to get out of prostituted situations.

In my nearly twenty years of work at Shared Hope, I've seen multiple occurrences of survivors who become involved with the movement without receiving the respect due to them, as Kristy mentioned she experienced. I've seen survivors invited to be speakers at events and not be compensated, while someone else at the same event who wrote a book and is thus considered "an expert" is well compensated. But who else can be a truer expert than those who've experienced this? Survivor voices are invaluable. They also have enough challenges overcoming their pasts and rebuilding new lives that they should be respected and listened to, and their potential recognized.

At Shared Hope, we've seen how essential it is to partner with or support survivors like Kristy in numerous aspects in seeking the most effective role in combating sex trafficking in the U.S. The movement could not meet the needs of victims without other survivors coming forward to bravely share their stories and do the hard work of rebuilding their lives.

With all of us working together, it is our greatest hope that someday our movement will become obsolete and no one is trafficked at all.

Until then, we'll keep working with people like Kristy who have come out of the darkness and are turning around to save others as well.

---

[1] Godwin, John. "Sex Work and the Law in Asia and the Pacific." United Nations Development Programme, http://www.undp.org/content/dam/undp/library/hivaids/English/HIV-2012-Sex-WorkAndLaw.pdf, October 2012.

[2] B. Julie Johnson, PhD. "Prostitution as 'Choice." *Ms. Magazine*, Jan/Feb, 1992. This was first published under the pseudonym "Jane Anthony" and was one of the first articles to educate people about the sex industry. It has been quoted a number of times by a well-known anti-trafficking leader who, after taking other material from the writer in 1996-97 and being confronted, has refused to cite any sources from her even when she uses them.

[3] Allen, Kelly. "Human Trafficking vs. Prostitution." https://blog.theexodusroad.com/human-trafficking-prostitution-difference, September 9, 2012.

[4] Kelleher, Susan. "Teen Missing after Testimony against Pimp." *Seattle Times*, Dec. 19, 2010; updated Dec. 20, 2010.

[5] *The Wichita Eagle*, June, 2018.

[6] *Reason*, April 10, 2017.

[7] Vivian Giang. "The Federal Government Is Reluctantly Teaming Up With Strip Clubs To Fight Sex Trafficking." *Business Insider*, Nov. 11, 2011.

22

THE ESSENTIAL
VOICES

Nancy Winston

For a long time, it seemed survivors were invisible. They were left in the shadows where people couldn't see or hear them. Or maybe people didn't want to see.

Sex trafficking is brutal and ugly and frightening, and in order to bring the brutality to light, we all must see it for the evil it is. We have to see and determine that the light will win over the darkness.

As a movement, our vision is what keeps us on course. Laws are complex, statistics are frightening, and the battle is exhausting. It is vision that keeps us going. Individuals and organizations involved in the anti-sex trafficking movement have one core vision that revolves around the deliverance of victims and survivors.

The fact is, an unknown number of girls and boys, women and men, do not survive sex trafficking. It is surely hundreds of thousands whose unheard cries are now forever silenced. Others who escape alive physically often remain dead inside, unable to find a therapeutic route from the abuse and trauma that was their "normal" so they build the sort of normal life the rest of us take for granted. We, who are the workers, thinkers, change-makers, and helpers in this movement, are haunted by these struggling souls and are driven by the need to uplift and empower those we can. Seeing lives that have been lost to death or to despair causes us to renew our vision and redouble our commitment to our core.

While the tragic loss of some reminds us that there is much more to do, it is the spirit of the survivor that inspires and informs our work and methods. This has been our most powerful weapon against the darkness — to learn and to listen to those who were in the shadows for so long.

My first understanding of domestic minor sex trafficking came from the young women and children in Mumbai, India. They were enslaved in large brothels and being sold to local men several times a day, every day. Regular police raids occurred, in the guise of fighting trafficking, but it was these victims who were arrested as prostitutes. They were then bailed out by the very enslavers who held them captive and then required to service even more clients to pay back their captors for the cost of bail.

The whole notion of prostituting child slaves was repulsive to me beyond words. But putting them in jail for the crime committed against them caused such outrage in me. The darkness was stifling in Mumbai; the shadows of terror and hopelessness were deep and wide.

The injustice was egregious. How could a civilized society sell its own women and children for sex, then make them the criminals instead of the men who were buying and selling them for pleasure and profit?

It was infuriating, and yet the depth of my horror was just beginning. I had no idea that another surprise awaited me as I returned to my own country. As I researched sex trafficking in the United States, I discovered the horrible truth — we were no different. American children were being sold for sex to American men. These kids were also prosecuted as criminals while the men (called by the common name of "john") regularly walked away from the crime scene. When pulled over or found by the police while they were committing child rape, they were given a ticket and drove away. They drove back to their lives, as if they'd been caught for speeding. The child was the one put in handcuffs, stuck into the back of the police car, taken to the jail, strip-searched, clothed in jail attire, locked behind bars, and later returned to the pimps with a new debt to pay and a criminal record to live with.

Today, law enforcement treats some of the children brutalized by traffickers and buyers as victims, but that is not yet a widespread attitude. Police officers still have the option to arrest children as prostitutes in the majority of states.

Why does this continue? Why do we treat our children like cattle while the men who buy them for sex pay their bill and move on? I believe we still have child prostitution laws on the books in so many states because bias against prostitution and the belief of complicity runs very deep in our society. Even today, it is this mindset that maintains laws that put kids in jail for being sold for sex.

It is here, in the shadows of anemic laws and widespread

ignorance, that we will continue to fight. We will call out the injustice, and we will continue to fight to change all of this. And we will do it with our most powerful weapon. Our key to reshaping culture and practice is alongside the survivors themselves.

Survivors — Voices that Matter

When I entered the fight to stop sex trafficking in the late 1990s, the voices of the girls, boys, women, and men who had endured, escaped, and survived these horrible crimes were often ignored or dismissed as fiction. A few courageous individuals were speaking out trying to tell the real story of what prostitution and domestic minor sex trafficking looked like, but very few were the survivors themselves. In the early days of the fight, the power these survivors carried with them wasn't recognized. But it would be their stories, told out in the open, that would finally shape the tide.

The voices of the survivors certainly shaped who I became as a leader. I gained my education through them. I've met these brave souls in over two decades of work around the globe; the thread of betrayal and pain in the stories of U.S. survivors varies little from those in India, Fiji, South Africa, Jamaica, The Netherlands, Amsterdam, Moldova, Nepal.

Many people who initially hear their stories here in the U.S. remain unconvinced, thinking something so brutal and unjust happening to so many *here in America* must be hyperbole. They listen and shake their heads and commend me for our work, but they don't realize the darkness is just over their own fence. Many simply will not believe that there are actual laws in the United States of America that blame children for being raped!

Did I discover this information from attorneys, judges, officers of the law? No. I discovered the inside information on the market from the very individuals who were first at the crime scene, the victims themselves.

As people wake up to the fact that this is happening in their neighborhoods, they are fighting against the darkness. Today, finally as a nation, we are doing more to give the respect and credibility due the survivor leaders in the movement. Some examples of this are seen in many areas, including:

- Survivors serving on the legislatively required survivor Advisory Council to the President of the United States
- They are becoming counselors, judges, and lawyers
- They are writing books to inform the general public on the real experiences of trafficking
- Survivors are mentoring other survivors in both formal and informal ways
- They are doing outreach in the places where they were once sold
- They are speaking out about the reality of what child sex trafficking does to the future of the child
- Some survivors are going to the prisons to reach out to women like them who were convicted of trafficking-related crimes
- They're becoming advisors to NGOs like Shared Hope International
- They advise on shelter management and procedures for DMST
- Survivors are becoming professional advisors to the courts

Still, more survivors need our help to become who they were made to be and fully overcome what's happened to them. Those who choose to publicly lead the fight need us to provide all the tools necessary to grow professionally. Many of us at Shared Hope have developed personal relationships with survivors. They affect our work on a daily basis by permitting us to glimpse the world through their unique experiences. They are our only way to understand and meet the needs of others.

A key person in our organization has consistently worked to ensure Shared Hope does not lose sight of our core vision — the deliverance of victims and survivors. Nancy Winston is one of those essential people who came along in a way we didn't plan or anticipate. Our lives crossed, and her heart and my vision made a connection that strengthened the very foundation of Shared Hope. It was in the early days of Shared Hope when I answered the phone and heard her voice for the first time. She'd seen a request in our newsletter for any donations that might help women build new lives. That desire to help survivors would become an unforeseen theme in Nancy's future.

Nancy worked in corporate America and wanted to donate some outdated computers to us. Being as Shared Hope was brand-new, the President and Founder was on phone duty the day she called, and while that surprised Nancy, our conversation also made an impression on me. So the next time I was in D.C., I took the train out to Nancy's house for dinner, still never guessing I had met a friend who would make an enormous impact on the work we do. Soon after that dinner, I ended up with my own guest room at Nancy's house to use during my travels to the Capitol. She traveled frequently as well with her job at Cerner Corporation, so she called my accommodations the B-no-B (bed, no breakfast)!

Nearly two decades later, Nancy is an integral part of Shared Hope. She's traveled with me to India and Nepal on numerous occasions, helping build Villages of Hope and bringing invaluable support and donations to the children there. She's served on the board at Shared Hope for six years, and upon retiring from her corporate career she became a Shared Hope employee. (She tells me she really enjoyed her one-week retirement!)

Desiring to gain more specific understanding of survivors' needs, Nancy pursued her Masters in Social Work and is currently a key advocate and support for survivors. Certainly, the journey from that phone call to where we are today has contributed to Shared Hope's deepening understanding of the survivor experience.

Here's Nancy to explain what she does, observes, and why she does it.

***

I guess I've always had a heart for survivors. I was horrified when I first learned what a pedophile was when my boys were 2 and 4. I thought, *Surely what I just read about is a very rare perversion.* But in the back of my mind, I knew it was not. That's probably what drew me to Shared Hope in the first place.

I received a mailing from Linda that talked about the children and women being sex trafficked in India. When I read it, my heart ached, and I wanted to do something. It's the same feeling I still have all these years later — a heart of compassion for the survivors. Gradually I became more and more involved with Shared

Hope, first as a volunteer and then more extensively as a board member, and now staff.

While there are many things we are trying to do, my piece has been focused on the men and women who were trafficked as kids.

One of my biggest goals is to help give a voice to those coming out of commercial sex trafficking. We have to listen to what they went through and really hear what they need — not always everything they want, but what they *need*. Each person is an individual, and trauma affects each one differently. To be heard, to be seen, to be accepted is what survivors need most. Even how we refer to them is important.

Support offered by others in the anti-trafficking movement who are not themselves survivors — and that includes most of us at Shared Hope — can be misguided or misunderstood. With good reason, survivors respond poorly to the word "rescue" because the word creates the connotation of weakness or something done to or for them. It conjures up the image of a rescued animal or someone who is a victim who lacks his or her own courage and fortitude. Quite the opposite is true! Just surviving the life of abuses they endured, much less moving on to an overcoming life, demonstrates just how much fortitude is really there.

I've learned that some object to the word "survivor," and some prefer "thriver" or "overcomer." While we wish to find the perfect name, everyone won't agree, so at some point we need a defined term to get services, to create understanding for those in our communities who have no idea sex trafficking is going on, and to be able to make changes.

What I know is that survivors need support to heal and

to carve out a life of their own. They need opportunities that were previously blocked to them.

Every organization in this movement has to define its role with regard to survivors. We have defined our role at Shared Hope as being a group that comes alongside them and becomes a friend to survivors. That is all we want to do. We try to provide these women and men with opportunities to develop individually and professionally.

We've done different work internationally where those forced into sex trafficking need literal rescue, and a few times that's been the case in the U.S. However, most of what we do is to assist survivors on a road toward empowerment. We want to give them exposure to opportunities that are going to help them get on a career or vocational path, pursue an education, or define their place in the anti-trafficking movement — whatever will help each individual.

One of the things that helps is getting them together at the JuST Conference we host every year. This is a chance for them to meet other survivors and see others like them in leading roles. They see the survivor presenters on stage and often reflect on or internalize how "That's something I'd like to do," or "I'd like to do something like that but in a different way." The conference opens a lot of eyes and inspires them to do something more. Similarly, our JuST Faith Summit, which is held bi-annually, provides

Shared Hope International annually hosts the Juvenile Sex Trafficking (JuST) Conference in locations around the United States. The conference continues to grow and gathers more than 1,000 people including survivors, professionals, and advocates. Many of the speakers are survivors.

a platform for survivor leaders who can share the impact of faith on their journey.

One transformed survivor is a woman I'll call "Mary." She had a history of trafficking and abuse that took place over many years. While she had received some services, she had no connections with other women who had also survived similar abuse, and the JuST Conference gave her that — her first experience. The first night was a survivors-only meet-and-greet, which proved to be overwhelming and triggering for Mary. I tried to comfort her but feared she might not want to continue the conference experience. Thankfully, other survivors proved to be the tonic she needed to add to her own courage and determination to carry on.

Each day I was happy to see she was still attending, and I could see her spirit lift visibly little by little. Slowly her expression softened. Then, I saw a smile!

After the event, she emailed saying that the conference meant so much to her.

"I've found my family," she wrote.

I have heard many times, "I didn't know other survivors were out there. I've never met another survivor or anyone who has been through what I've been through." This is especially true with the small but growing number of male survivors. One man, a professional who was joining for the first time as a presenter and as a survivor, said he was more nervous about attending the survivor networking event than he was about his presentation. But once again, it was the survivor community to the rescue, and soon he felt very much at home. These are just a few examples of why it's so important for us to create opportunities for more survivors to come find that place of belonging. It's also why we try to raise donations to bring more new people in. In 2017, we had more than a hundred survivors attend the conference, with thirty-five of them giving plenary addresses or leading workshops. That's a huge turn from the days when survivors were marginalized and often ignored. Their voices are finally being heard.

While there are always challenges, we ask the survivors and ourselves every year, *How can we make it a better environment next time?* We reassess and are constantly learning from our mistakes and from the honest feedback from these experts.

It is not clean and simple forming relationships with people who have endured a unique form of trauma that I have never personally experienced. I can never hope to have sufficient understanding, and the gulf that separates us always challenges me. I am left with deep admiration for survivors' resilience, their passion and ideas, their strength of will. I am especially thankful for those who embrace the good, if imperfect, intentions of people like me.

At Shared Hope, we'll continue to do all we can to help the survivors become all God made them to be, and to nurture the strength and talents they have. Just as in the beginning, they have my heart.

23

A LOOK AT THE WINS

THE WINS KEEP US ALL GOING.

Today there are innumerable groups, non-governmental organizations, church ministries, and individuals trying to save kids from the streets, restore their futures, and obtain justice for them. America continues to wake up to the problem. Stories are being told, and communities are inspired to rise up and insist that this stop.

The subject of human trafficking has been captured on episodes of TV shows like *CSI* and *Law & Order*, on made-for-TV-movies, and on major films on the big screen. Across the country, events are held, and posters are hung in airports, shopping centers, gas stations, and truck stops. Shared Hope and other organizations are providing valuable training across the nation and around the world. People who work for schools, hospitals, the hospitality industry, airlines, and even service industries like Uber are hearing about the signs and dangers of trafficking.

And it's all making a difference. The online Goliath looms large and powerful, but the wins are like stones in David's slingshot. The wins keep us all going.

Survivor Voices Heard

When President Barack Obama made the appointment of the United States Advisory Council on Human Trafficking in 2015, further progress and empowerment for survivors was made. The eleven survivors, now members of the Council, were not being viewed as former prostitutes, but as women and men worthy to be listened to at the highest levels of U.S. government.

The members represented a diverse range of backgrounds and experiences and were then able to advise and make recommendations on federal anti-trafficking policies. To acknowledge survivor leaders as a key component in initiatives for change is to empower them to be a voice for the most vulnerable in the world of human trafficking. They know more than anyone what is needed to address the many issues that contribute to the long-standing existence of human trafficking in the United States and around the world. They became voices of the voiceless.

There are survivors today who have made such strides that they run nonprofits, testify at Senate hearings, influence legislative changes, speak across the country, and help save other victims of child sex trafficking.

The Vacatur laws offer hope to regain both a sense of justice and the freedom from a criminal record that is undeserved for victims.

National Impact

In most every state, laws and policies and perceptions have changed. Through the FBI, the National Center for Missing and Exploited Children, and the U.S. Department of Justice, the numbers are a revelation of the problem and a triumph of their efforts. Through the work of federal agencies with the Innocence Lost Initiative there have been:

- More than 2,100 children rescued
- Over 1,000 traffickers and facilitators convicted that included life sentences and assets seizure

Since its inception in 2006, Project Safe Childhood has had:

- Nearly 11,500 convictions in federal courts for offenses related to the sexual exploitation of a minor
- 2,500 children identified in images (video and photographs) of children in sexually exploited situations

On the Project Safe Childhood website, lists of convictions are updated frequently. They depict the successful prosecutions of sexual offenses against children whether the court sentencing was carried out or not.

Today, there are more arrests of traffickers and buyers and higher conviction rates than ever before.

Between May 1, 2010, and May 1, 2015, the U.S. Marshals Service (USMS) opened 16,320 investigations of convicted sex offenders for violations of Adam Walsh Child Protection and Safety Act (AWA) and arrested 2,671 individuals on federal sex offender registration charges. USMS closed by arrest 23,986 state/

local warrants charging failure to register during that period, based on USMS's investigations, federal prosecutors obtained 2,375 convictions.[1]

Amy O'Neill Richard is still at work at the U.S. Department of State in the Trafficking in Person's office after receiving that first call more than fifteen years ago. In that time, the staff at the TIP office has increased from six or seven people to more than sixty employees dedicated to monitoring and combatting trafficking in the United States and around the world. There are state laws in various forms of sufficiency in nearly all states that are meant to help victims and not treat them as offenders, and anti-trafficking task forces have been initiated across the country.

For the full list of countries, go to the United Nations' website treaty status of United Nations Convention against Transnational Organized Crime.

Ernie Allen retired from NCMEC and ICMEC. However, instead of packing up and returning to his beloved Kentucky to enjoy retirement, Ernie has been busier than ever. He has become an advisor to Shared Hope International as well as other organizations. He's worked with the Vatican on ways to stop child sex trafficking, as well as with the British government and Prime Minister David Cameron — even major tech companies in the UK — on ways to protect children from the availability of pornography and from online predators.

Meanwhile, NCMEC continues to develop ways to help find missing and exploited children through any means possible, including the latest in technological apps and helps.

Sting Operations

At Super Bowl XLVII in 2014, as the Seattle Seahawks beat the Denver Broncos, law enforcement conducted a sting operation. They arrested 45 pimps and rescued 25 child victims of human trafficking.

The next year's Super Bowl brought the culmination of a nationwide sting operation over the course of several weeks. During one called *National Day of Johns*, 600 people were arrested and 68 victims were rescued.

During the summer of 2017, more than 1,000 people were arrested in a month-long nationwide sex-trafficking sting operation.

CYBERTIPLINE

From the Justice Department website:

"Since the inception of its CyberTipline in 1998, NCMEC (National Center for Missing and Exploited Children) has processed more than 8.4 million reports (nearly half of those in 2015) related to incidents of child sexual exploitation, the majority of which relate to activities connected to child pornography and the internet. Since the CyberTipline was created, NCMEC has seen a dramatic increase in the number of reports received."[2]

In one *Time* magazine article about a successful sting operation, Cook County Sheriff Tom Dart said, "If there was no demand, there would be no prostitution."

He followed saying, "It makes them understand that there are some consequences here. The public still perceives prostitution as a victimless crime, so we're going about it this way to address the problem and raise awareness."

These numbers may be easy to skim over or look at nominally, but when we pause and really think about the individual lives, those numbers become more impactful. Thousands of convictions. And 2,500 individual children identified as exploited victims.

As soldiers in the fight against human trafficking, we continue to meet over dinner, coffee, around conference tables in offices in D.C. or around the country where we all may be pulled together for an event or fundraiser. When I see Drew or Ernie, or I come into the office and see Samantha or Christine or other staff of Shared Hope, when I'm staying at "my" room at Nancy's house in Maryland, we gather for essentially one purpose — to see the end of child sex trafficking in America, and worldwide.

Whether we are attorneys, government employees, appointed officials, law enforcement, or concerned citizens, we have a common fight, and a common purpose.

There are innumerable faces and names I wish to include in this book. So many others are running their NGOs, serving as elected officials, signing up as Defenders online, sitting in malls handing out brochures to get the word out, trying to help homeless, easy-target youth out on the streets.

For all the days and weeks and months that Shared Hope International employees and volunteers spend researching and reaching out, there are hundreds of others — like trained Ambassadors of Hope, who press against the barriers in their own communities and states to fight for the freedom of children caught up in the dark world of domestic minor sex trafficking.

Late-night discussions, intense planning, fundraisers, sting operations, movie productions, and so much more, all require long hours of preparation and implementation for creating a tidal wave of change across our great nation.

In January 2017, I met with two moms who'd come to Washington, D.C., to speak at a Senate hearing against Backpage. com, the second largest classified ad listing online in the United States. Backpage.com offered listings for a wide variety of products and services, but these two mothers were here for particular products it had facilitated the sale of: their teenage daughters.

These moms, who had cried countless tears and felt their hearts ripped to pieces again and again, somehow found the strength to speak out about the devastating consequences that sex trafficking had on their own children and families.

They were calling Backpage.com and its executives to account for providing a place where traffickers could profit from the sale of underage victims. At this Senate hearing, they clearly spoke to the leaders of our nation and described how their girls and their families would never be the same. They stood up against the terrors that nearly destroyed the lives of their daughters.

That night after dinner, I took these two women over to the Capitol for an after-hours exploration of the halls and rooms. We walked where U.S. Presidents have walked and stood beneath the dome looking up at *The Apotheosis of Washington*, painted in 1865 right after the Civil War.

I watched these warrior women gather themselves after the hearing, and I watched them walk the halls and corridors of that enormous building. They snapped pictures, smiled, laughed. They marveled at the beauty and significance. They pointed to statues and paintings of other women who had stood up for their beliefs. Together, we crossed floors and moved through rooms that were the wheels of government for our country for 200 years. We stood where President John F. Kennedy's casket had sat during his internment and walked to a plaque on the floor that marked where President Abraham Lincoln's desk once sat.

In this place where politicians and representatives of all the U.S. citizens come together to create laws and make change, this place was for them.

We do have Goliaths to face. But we have our wins, and for those we must celebrate.

We have rescued children, helped restore lives, and seen justice carried out. The progress offers an incentive and reward to keep going. It offers continued hope. A hope that we all can share in.

I can envision thousands of people I've met over the years across this great nation and around the world who were fighting sex trafficking, learning about it, or escaping from it. They are diplomats and leaders in foreign countries. They are U.S. politicians and government employees. They are law enforcement officers and church volunteers. They are parents and they are survivors. Every gender, race, background, career, and religion can be represented.

I also see the survivors and victims still out there. While we celebrate the triumphs, we keep going for those who still need us.

All of this work is worth it.

They are worth it.

---

[1] "Fact Sheet: Project Safe Childhood." The U.S. Department of Justice. https://www.justice.gov/psc/file/842426/download.

[2] "Fact Sheet: Project Safe Childhood." The U.S. Department of Justice, https://www.justice.gov/psc/file/842426/download.

A Look at the Wins

24

LIGHTS IN THE DARKNESS

B ack in 1910 when The Mann Act was passed, the crusaders were intent on ending the practice of "white slavery." This term was used to get the word out, to wake America up. Today, we disagree with such terminologies or exclusions with no mention of other ethnic groups yet we can read how their intentions for these young women were sincere. These were people living in an era only fifty years beyond the Civil War and the Emancipation Proclamation. Women wouldn't get the right to vote for another decade. Civil rights, women's rights, and human rights were far off in the future.

While it was a different time, the fight remains the same.

Today, we have a different course and battle plan.

We are tackling Demand as never before.

We are pushing states to change their laws and practices to protect kids found in these situations, and to give them help and services as victims instead of prosecution as criminals.

Survivors are not considered women who were led into an immoral life as those in 1910 viewed them. We call them overcomers, former victims who triumphed, and experts in their field.

Today, we face giants unseen before in time and history with the invention of the Internet. Children aren't out on the street corners now; they're bought and sold over smart phones and computers and all around the globe. They are delivered to the privacy of houses and apartments instead of back alleys and local parks. We battle tech companies whose products aid in the facilitation of the trafficking of children, and who choose profit over kids' lives. While we can use tech tools to save children, since the trade has moved online, the advantage remains greatly against us.

Yet we battle on. Just as a shepherd boy faced a giant thousands of years ago, so we too go forward to face things bigger than we are. The people in this book, and thousands of others out there fighting to stop this deplorable industry, won't stand down or give up.

And we ask for you to join us.

In 1910, people like you and me stood up for victims of sex trafficking, changed a law, and started a movement to save young women. There is a large gap in that progress, but it's advancing rapidly now. For the last two decades, America has been waking up — and not just to look around, but to do something about it.

Goliaths continue to roam the land. We still have much to do. But together, we can save future generations of children, help restore the victims of today, get justice for the victims, and make the world a much better place.

LIGHTS IN THE DARKNESS

We will continue to invade the darkness, and we challenge you to invade the darkness in your community of influence as well.

DMST TIMELINE

DOMESTIC MINOR SEX TRAFFICKING (DMST) HISTORICAL TIMELINE

U.S. LEGISLATION & KEY ACTIONS

1910 – The Mann Act, also called the White Slave Traffic Act
The Mann Act and its subsequent amendment resolutions make it a felony to knowingly persuade, induce, entice, or coerce an individual to travel across state lines to engage in prostitution or attempt to do so.

1935 – Child Welfare Services Program established under Title IV-B of the Social Security Act
Through the Child Welfare Services Program, the federal government started providing grants to states for preventive and protective services and foster care payments.

1970 – Racketeer Influenced and Corrupt Organizations Act (RICO)
Enacted as part of the Organized Crime Control Act of 1970, RICO expanded criminal penalties that reach all of parties involved in a criminal enterprise and provided a civil cause of action for those injured by RICO violations. The Trafficking

Victims Protection Reauthorization Act of 2003 amended the definition of "racketeering activity" to include sex and labor trafficking.

1974 – Child Abuse Prevention and Treatment Act (CAPTA)

CAPTA provides federal funding to states in support of prevention, assessment, investigation, prosecution, and treatment activities and also provides program grants to public agencies and nonprofit organizations, including Indian Tribes and Tribal organizations. In 2015, the Justice for Victims of Trafficking Act amended CAPTA to expand the definition of an abused and neglected child to include child sex-trafficking victims as defined under 22 USC 7012, the Trafficking Victims Protection Act.

1974 – Juvenile Justice & Delinquency Prevention Act

Provides funds to states that follow a series of federal protections, known as the "core protections," on the care and treatment of youth in the justice system. Created the Office of Juvenile Justice & Delinquency Prevention (OJJDP) within the U.S. Department of Justice. Along with CAPTA and RHYA, this statute establishes some of the primary federal funding streams that are used to serve DMST youth through existing state child-serving systems.

1974 – Runaway and Homeless Youth Act (RHYA)

Originally enacted as Title III of the Juvenile Justice & Delinquency Prevention Act, RHYA established the federal definition of "homeless youth" and formed the basis for the Runaway and Homeless Youth Program administered by the Family and Youth Services Bureau at the U.S. Department of Health and Human Services and provides federal funding for emergency shelters and other services targeted at runaway and homeless youth.

1982 – Missing Children Act

Authorized the FBI to enter and maintain relevant information about missing children in the National Crime Information Center (NCIC). Enabled law enforcement from the federal, state, and local levels to access this information, providing a previously lacking resource for finding a missing child.

1983 – Missing Children's Assistance Act

Amended the Juvenile Justice and Delinquency Prevention Act of 1974 to require the Administrator of OJJDP to establish and maintain a national toll-free telephone line for reporting information regarding the location of missing children and to establish a national resource center and clearinghouse on missing children. OJJDP delegated these mandates to the National Center for Missing & Exploited Children.

1984 – National Center for Missing & Exploited Children

Opened by President Ronald Reagan on June 13, 1984, to serve as the national resource center and clearinghouse for missing and exploited children and operate the national toll-free missing children's hotline.

1984 – Victims of Crime Act

Established the Office for Victims of Crime at the U.S. Department of Justice that administers the Crime Victims Fund, which is financed by fines paid by convicted federal offenders. These funds may be distributed to states for victim compensation and grants supporting victim services, as well as other purposes. VOCA funds are available to Child Advocacy Centers serving human-trafficking victims.

1987 – Child Exploitation & Obscenity Section, U.S. Department of Justice

Specialized prosecutorial unit created within the Justice Department's Criminal Division to enforce federal criminal statutes relating to the exploitation of children and obscenity.

1990 – Crime Control Act

Major legislation that had substantial impact on juvenile crime control policies of the 1990s. The act made major changes in the areas of child abuse, sexual abuse penalties, and victim rights.

1990 – National Child Search Assistance Act

A title of the Crime Control Act, this act required local, state, and federal law enforcement agencies to immediately enter information about abducted children into the National Crime Information Center (NCIC) database without requiring a waiting period, ending the long-standing law enforcement practice of a mandatory waiting period in missing child cases.

1994 – Violence Against Women Act

Provided $1.6 billion toward investigation and prosecution of violent crimes against women, including victims of human trafficking. It also imposed automatic and mandatory restitution on those convicted and allowed civil redress in cases prosecutors chose to leave unprosecuted; established the Office on Violence Against Women within the U.S. Department of Justice.

1994 – The Violent Crime Control and Law Enforcement Act of 1994

A massive bill providing for 100,000 new police officers, $9.7 billion in funding for prisons and $6.1 billion in funding for prevention programs. It included the Jacob Wetterling Crimes Against Children Registration Act, which mandated states to establish registries for sexual offenders and created a number of new federal crimes including hate crimes, sex crimes, and gang-related crimes.

1996 – World Congress on the Commercial Sexual Exploitation of Children

Held in Stockholm, Sweden, the first World Congress sought to draw attention to the plight of children in the world sex trade and devise strategies to protect children from sexual exploitation. It was followed by the Second World Congress in Yokohama, Japan, in 2001 and a Third World Congress in Rio De Janeiro, Brazil, in 2008.

1998 – Establishment of the CyberTipline

Congress funded the creation of a 24-hour mechanism for reporting tips and leads online regarding the sexual exploitation of children. The CyberTipline is housed at the National Center for Missing & Exploited Children.

1998 – Creation of the Internet Crimes Against Children Task Force Initiative (ICAC)

Congress began to fund multi-jurisdictional (federal, state, local) law enforcement task forces nationwide to combat the sexual exploitation of children.

2000 – United Nations Protocols

Three protocols were adopted by the United Nations to supplement the 2000 Convention Against Transnational Organized Crime (the Palermo Protocols). The protocols and convention fall within the jurisdiction of the United Nations Office on Drugs and Crime. Of particular importance were the Protocol to Prevent, Suppress, and Punish Trafficking in Persons, especially Women and Children and the Protocol Against Smuggling Migrants by Land, Sea, or Air. The United States ratified both protocols in 2000. Later, the U.S. ratified the Optional Protocol on the Sale of Children, Child Prostitution, and Child Pornography in 2002, which prohibits the commercial sexual exploitation of children and protects them from being sold for any purpose.

2000 – Trafficking Victims Protection Act of 2000

The first comprehensive federal law to address trafficking in persons. TVPA updated post-Civil War slavery statutes, furthering the guarantees of freedom from slavery and involuntary servitude set forth in the U.S. Constitution and articulated in the Universal Declaration of Human Rights. It also reauthorized federal programs to prevent violence against women. TVPA was reauthorized by Congress in 2003, 2005, 2008, and 2013. In 2008 it was renamed the William Wilberforce Trafficking Victims Reauthorization Act, and in 2013 it was reauthorized as part of the Violence Against Women Reauthorization Act.

2000 – Office to Monitor and Combat Trafficking in Persons, U.S. Department of State

Pursuant to the Trafficking Victims Protection Act of 2000, the U.S. State Department established the Office to Monitor and Combat Trafficking in Persons (TIP Office), which partners with foreign governments, international organizations, civil society, and the private sector to develop and implement effective strategies for confronting modern slavery. The office issues an annual Trafficking in Persons Report to assess and place each country in a tier ranking with non-humanitarian funding suspension as an enforcement tool. The first report was issued in 2001.

2001 – War Against Trafficking Alliance

HR 2500, the Departments of Commerce, Justice, and State, the Judiciary, and Related Agencies Appropriations Act, 2002, included significant funds to convene an international conference on combating sex trafficking. The conferees expected the newly established Office to Monitor and Combat Trafficking in Persons to oversee the conference as a public/private partnership, and SHI Founder Linda Smith initiated the formation of the War Against Trafficking Alliance to be the partner on the conference. Other leaders in the alliance included International Justice Mission, Salvation Army, and the Johns Hopkins School of International Studies Protection Project. In 2003, the World Summit, titled Pathbreaking Strategies in the Global Fight Against Sex Trafficking, convened activists from 114 countries to discuss practical solutions to the problems of sex tourism and trafficking. Six international Next Steps Conferences were later held as a follow-up to the World Summit funded by the appropriations for the State Department to assist other international cooperative efforts to fight trafficking in persons.

2003 – Prosecutorial Remedies and Other Tools to End the Exploitation of Children Today (PROTECT ACT OF 2003)

Enhanced sentencing of sex offenders, provided for criminal history background checks for volunteer organizations, eliminated statutes of limitation for child abuse, created a national AMBER Alert System, eliminated waiting periods for missing 18- to 21-year-olds, prohibited virtual child pornography, prohibited U.S. citizens from engaging in illicit sexual conduct abroad (child sex tourism), created mandatory minimum sentences for certain crimes, and much more.

2003 – Innocence Lost National Initiative

A joint initiative launched in 2003 by the FBI, U.S. Department of Justice Child Exploitation and Obscenity Section, and the National Center for Missing & Exploited Children targeting domestic minor sex trafficking. It involved the creation of multi-jurisdictional task forces nationwide and periodic national sweeps called Operation Cross Country designed to rescue exploited children and arrest traffickers.

2005 – National Human Trafficking Hotline

The National Human Trafficking Hotline was established as a 24-hour confidential, multi-lingual hotline for victims, survivors, and witnesses of human trafficking. The hotline was a component of the first awareness campaign implemented by public relations firm Ketchum, and the national human-trafficking hotline was built and operated by Lockheed Martin and Covenant House; in 2007, operation shifted to Polaris Project, where it continues under a grant from DHHS.

2006 – Adam Walsh Child Protection and Safety Act of 2006

Established a national sex offender registry and requirements for state registries. Created three tiers for convicted sex offenders based upon the crime committed. Also amended the National Child Search Assistance Act of 1990 to require law enforcement to enter information about missing and abducted children into the NCIC database within two hours of receiving a report.

2006 – Project Safe Childhood

A nationwide initiative to combat child sexual exploitation and abuse launched in May 2006 by the U.S. Department of Justice. Led by the U.S. Attorneys' Offices and the Criminal Division's Child Exploitation and Obscenity Section (CEOS), Project Safe Childhood marshals federal, state, and local resources to better locate, apprehend, and prosecute individuals who exploit children via the Internet, as well as to identify and rescue victims.

2006 – United States Mid-Term Review on the Commercial Sexual Exploitation of Children

Conducted by Shared Hope International, ECPAT USA and The Protection Project at Johns Hopkins School of Advanced International Studies, the Mid-Term Review gathered stakeholders from across the country to measure progress by the U.S. in addressing the goals of the Second World Congress Against Commercial Sexual Exploitation of Children in 2001 in Yokohama, Japan, and the adoption of the Optional Protocol on the Rights of the Child on the Sale of Children. The resulting report was submitted to the Third World Congress in Rio de Janeiro, Brazil, together with the separate U.S.-Canada Mid-Term Review for the World Congress Against Commercial Sexual Exploitation of Children also conducted by SHI and ECPAT USA. The process demonstrated the breadth of the definition of DMST to include the various forms of commercial sexual exploitation of children and encouraged stakeholders to see all forms as a crime and the children as victims of a crime.

2006 – Domestic Minor Sex Trafficking Defined

As a result of SHI research for the U.S. Department of State on trafficking markets in several countries including the United States, titled *Demand*, funding is designated for SHI to work with the Department of Justice Bureau of Justice Assistance (BJA) to design and implement local assessments of the systems in place to identify and facilitate access to services for victims of domestic child sex trafficking, and to work with the federally funded human-trafficking task forces in ten locations to increase awareness and responses to this crime. The term "Domestic Minor Sex Trafficking" was established to distinguish this unique type of human trafficking to improve identification and response systems.

2008 – Protecting Children from Pornography & Internet Exploitation Act of 2008 (PROTECT ACT OF 2008)

Required the Department of Justice to develop and implement a National Strategy for Child Exploitation Prevention and Interdiction, improve the Internet Crimes Against Children Task Forces, increase resources for computer forensic labs, and improve the investigation and prosecution of child predators. Mandated placement of a National Coordinator within the U.S. Department of Justice to author and coordinate the strategy. The first National Strategy was published in 2011.

Oct. 21, 2009 – International Violence Against Women: Stories and Solutions Hearing before the Subcommittee On International Organizations, Human Rights And Oversight of the Committee on Foreign Affairs House Of Representatives (111th Congress, First Session)

Highlighted the International Violence Against Women's Act (IVAWA), a crucial piece of legislation that would direct more attention and resources to efforts to halt gender-based violence that affects women and girls around the globe, including sex trafficking for the first time. SHI Founder Linda Smith testified to the problem of domestic sex trafficking resource disparity.

Dec. 22, 2009 – S. 2925 (111th): Domestic Minor Sex Trafficking Deterrence and Victims Support Act of 2010

Motivated by the research done on domestic minor sex trafficking and published in The National Report, Senator Ron Wyden introduced this comprehensive bill to increase and focus funding on the prevention and response to DMST. Though it was passed by both chambers on December 21, 2010, it was passed in non-identical forms and the differences were never resolved. It was reintroduced as S. 596 (112th), the Domestic Minor Sex Trafficking Deterrence and Victims Support Act of 2011, on March 16, 2011. It was never enacted in whole but provisions of this bill were incorporated into other bills.

Sept. 15, 2010 – Domestic Minor Sex Trafficking Hearing before the House of Representatives, Subcommittee On Crime, Terrorism, And Homeland Security Committee on the Judiciary

SHI's two research reports and findings on domestic sex trafficking of children, the "Domestic Minor Sex Trafficking: Prostituting American Children" and "Demand," are introduced into the Congressional Record.

2011 – OJJDP Grant Solicitation for Technical Assistance to Programs to Address Commercial Sexual Exploitation (CSE)/ Domestic Minor Sex Trafficking (DMST)

This initiative marked the first use of the term DMST in external programming by the Department of Justice signifying an understanding of the unique nature of the crime. This FY2011 grant funds an organization to provide technical assistance to OJJDP grantees and other organizations addressing CSE or DMST of girls and boys. The program offers education and training, expert consultations, peer-to-peer networking opportunities, resources, and other tailored assistance to respond to diverse communities concerning the sexual victimization of girls and boys.

2011 – Protected Innocence Challenge Report Cards

In a parallel event at the National Association of Attorneys General Winter Meeting, SHI launches the Protected Innocence Challenge, issuing individual state legislative analyses and report card annually to grade each state on its laws related to domestic minor sex trafficking. In the first year, 26 states fail the Protected Innocence Challenge.

2012 – National Colloquium: Shelter and Services Evaluation for Action

Experts convene from around the nation at the U.S. Capitol for a discussion hosted by SHI, the Congressional Caucus for Victim's Rights and the Congressional Caucus for Women's Issues. The resulting report distills perspectives from over 100 provider, survivor, government, advocacy, and funding experts on trends and barriers to secure restorative shelter and services for juvenile sex trafficking victims. The Colloquium is held again in 2013 and 2014 and becomes the foundation for the permanent JuST Response Council generating consensus on policies and definitions within the child sex trafficking field to limit the diversifying application of the law.

2013 – *United States v. Jungers* and *United States v. Bonestroo*

A joint decision in these cases — which were brought against attempted buyers of sex with children who were caught in a sting operation in South Dakota and prosecuted under the federal sex-trafficking law — was the first appellate decision to confirm that the federal sex-trafficking law reached the conduct of buyers. The decision in these cases established a critical precedent that clarified the role of buyers in the crime of sex trafficking. In 2015, the Eighth Circuit's decision was codified by Congress in the Justice for Victims of Trafficking Act to prevent this important decision from being undermined by a potential circuit split.

2014 – Preventing Sex Trafficking and Strengthening Families Act

With evidence that large numbers of sex-trafficked children were or are in the foster care system, this law requires data collection and reporting by states on identification of children who may be at high-risk of becoming sex-trafficking victims, particularly current and former foster children. It also establishes a National Advisory Committee on the Sex Trafficking of Children and Youth in the U.S. to advise on policies to improve the nation's response to the sex trafficking of children and youth and to make recommendations for administrative and legislative changes to which key experts from SHI and other advocacy organizations are appointed. The council convened its first public meeting in September 2018, and its first report to Congress is due January 20, 2019.

2015 – Justice for Victims of Trafficking Act

With empirical evidence of the low rate of prosecutions of buyers of sex with children published in the Demanding Justice Report by SHI in 2014, the JVTA is enacted with a critical provision clarifying the federal sex-trafficking statute's application to actions by buyers, specifically "patronize and solicits," codifying the decision in United States v. Jungers, 702 F.3d 1066 (8th Cir. 2013). It provides more services for victims, deprives convicted offenders of criminal assets, uses forfeited assets to satisfy restitution orders for victims, and gives law enforcement better tools to fight sex trafficking. Also created a United States Advisory Council on Human Trafficking with a mandate to review and recommend policy and programs on human trafficking, report to senior administration and agency officials, and submit a report to the President's Interagency Task Force to Monitor and Combat Trafficking in Persons.

2015 – International Megan's Law

Focusing on the challenge of child sex tourism, this law created an Angel Watch Center within the U.S. Department of Homeland Security to receive notifications regarding convicted sex offenders preparing to travel, as well as alerts from other countries regarding convicted sex offenders traveling to the U.S. It also promotes information sharing between countries and law enforcement.

2015 – Office of Trafficking in Persons established as a separate office within the Department of Health and Human Services

Acknowledging the prevalence of domestic human trafficking and the impact on survivors and lack of services available for the domestic population, the Office of Trafficking in Persons (Tip Office) was created. Previously, the Office of Refugee Resettlement (ORR) was the office within HHS that responded to human-trafficking victims, despite its focus on international trafficking and the recognized increase in domestic trafficking.

2018 – Allow States and Victims to Fight Online Sex Trafficking Act (FOSTA-SESTA)

HR 1865, the Allow States and Victims to Fight Online Sex Trafficking Act, also known as FOSTA-SESTA, is signed into law after years of failed lawsuits by survivors of sex trafficking who were sold for sex online, especially on Backpage. com. FOSTA-SESTA amends Section 230 to allow state prosecutions and allow civil claims to proceed by victims.

Renting Lacy: A Story of America's Prostituted Children

by Linda Smith

Based on actual encounters, Linda exposes the underworld of child sex trafficking in America by telling the stories of those who live there, the traffickers, the buyers, and the victims who struggle to survive each night.

Learn how you can take action and make a difference! Request your copy at **sharedhope.org**.